T0381117

Violet has a message for all who find this book. We are all in a fight, an invisible fight for our life force aka soul. I urge you to see it this way in even the smallest of ways. The ways our soul gets hijacked are many. People, food, drugs, poor thinking habits are all ways they siphon your energy. Be mindful of your power and how valuable you are. Each and every soul is valuable beyond estimation. You must discern, clean your body, wake up to the reality that your whole being is sought after by the dark. Toxins are the biggest culprit, as tv, phones, music are all distractions that use radiation to weaken and lower your frequencies. If you choose to stand in your warrior soul position, let this be your guide and assurance that GOD will assist you. It is really that simple, begin to build your relationship with your inner warrior.

*"You are protected and loved. You are a true miracle and now is the time to awaken into your full and true energies."*

— Violet Light

# GOD

## *Is*

# WATER

*Water is Thicker than Blood*

## VIOLET LIGHT

**BALBOA.**PRESS
A DIVISION OF HAY HOUSE

Balboa Press books may be ordered through booksellers or by contacting:

Balboa Press
A Division of Hay House
1663 Liberty Drive
Bloomington, IN 47403
www.balboapress.com
844-682-1282

Because of the dynamic nature of the Internet, any web addresses or links contained in this book may have changed since publication and may no longer be valid. The views expressed in this work are solely those of the author and do not necessarily reflect the views of the publisher, and the publisher hereby disclaims any responsibility for them.

Scripture quotations marked NLT are taken from the Holy Bible, New Living Translation, copyright © 1996, 2004, 2007. Used by permission of Tyndale House Publishers, Inc. Carol Stream, Illinois 60188. All rights reserved. Website

Any people depicted in stock imagery provided by Getty Images are models, and such images are being used for illustrative purposes only.
Certain stock imagery © Getty Images.

Print information available on the last page.

ISBN: 979-8-7652-4827-0 (sc)
ISBN: 979-8-7652-4828-7 (e)

Library of Congress Control Number: 2024900068

Interior Graphics/Art Credit: Violet Light

Balboa Press rev. date: 03/05/2024

# CONTENTS

# FORWARD/ DEDICATIONS

I am dedicating this book to all of my ancestors. They are the ones that led me here **to** this very moment in time. I realize we are all called to a destiny on the Earth. I realize how rare it is to be born, to be born in America and to be still alive after fifty-four years. I have no words to describe the honor and gratitude I have to live here. I know the suffering I have endured has created a truth in me. The actual truth is who I am. The learning that takes place here or I shall say the remembering is fantastic. I love the idea of growing older to sit in the wisest seat of humanity. There is an African proverb that says, "When an old person dies, a library burns down".

I also dedicate this book to Dr. Tom Norris. He saved me just in the nick of time. I was so scared and confused. I was willing to release my physical body to a hospital to seek a cure. I know now that confusion is the realm of the dark entities that seek to obtain your soul. I am so grateful he manifested into my life and released the souls to the infinite light. In doing so he taught me how to continue to heal lost souls. Dr. Norris and I experienced the most amazing phenomenon to date, no other documented cases have been found. He witnessed me being zapped by the light of source. In that moment we created a portal to the light that has carried me through all of the trauma and suffering I have endured. I am able to forgive all of those who have trespassed against me. I seek to heal as many souls I can. I am protected by this great love frequency and it feels so peaceful. I wish for all of you reading this that you seek this connection.

I wish to thank all of the masters of light that are by my side healing and guiding me. I am so lucky to be in communication. I hear with my intuition so clearly now, as I am one with my spiritual tribe. It is an honor to be called to this realm to experience truth, beauty and love. Fear does not exist here.

I thank all of you who read my testament to the love of our GOD. You will be drawn to this book in accordance to your highest destiny. If you were not aware that you are guided and protected as to your distinct and unique journey, be aware now. You have a group of guides that assist you with your life tasks and lessons. It is up to each soul here to open the portals to listen. These guides cannot interfere or change your path, they can only assist you when you are stuck or going the wrong way. They will hold you in times of deep pain and sorrow.

Unfortunately, wisdom mostly comes with age. The distractions here, keep us in the illusion that life is not a gift, that we are owed something. I am so glad to see through this falsehood. I expect to break free from all of the illusions as my time passes here. I know from all I have experienced, I was deeply loved and needed here. My intention is to help even one human understand that suffering is all part of our journey. Suffering is not in vain, so view it as a blessing. I would learn later that this is a Buddhist belief. Turn the script around and thank God for your suffering. I can attest that so much good has come out of my most traumatic moments. If you choose to seek them out, you will make all of the connections.

One beautiful example I read was about two sisters who were prisoners in a Nazi concentration camp. They were assigned to a dormitory crawling with lice and fleas. They read the scripture Thessalonians 5:16:18 "Give thanks in all circumstances" and they prayed and thanked God for the lice. The other women overheard them praising God for the lice and asked why would you thank God for the pests that are torturing us? The sisters followed the word and prayed everyday thanking God.

All in the ward were spared physical and sexual abuse from the guards due to the lice. Amen

Life right now seems more difficult than ever before. The new standard of disasters, death, inflation, fear of imminent wars, all have our souls shaken up. Yet again, another illusion of the dark forces. We can never be in poverty or lack if our mind is in complete faith. It truly is the only way out of all the chaos. Many are experiencing this and will attest to having complete faith in God. Miracles are happening and those who believe will find the bliss in the light. I have touched the light and it is like being *electrocuted by love.* I will attest on the mountain tops that the love awaiting us after this dimension, will be all you need. It is my testament that when we leave here, we will be loved like nothing we ever knew on this planet.

The secret is that your soul knows this already and that is why keep trying to find it here. Perhaps some will come close. I believe I have many times It is no comparison to what I experienced that beautiful November day in 1996, a holy, ethereal, electrifying cosmic blast to my heart chakra.

This is what we all are seeking again and again. Know that this love is awaiting you. Choose it, desire it and will it, as it is naturally yours. Water saved my life; God saved my life. God is Water! Water is consciousness. Water is mentioned a total of 722 times in the Bible, more often than faith, hope, prayer, and worship.

Violet Light

# A WARRIOR BORN

Down the rabbit hole of life, I fell. I went tumbling, flipping, scraping the sides until I crash landed into a hell of pain, suffering, disconnect, great loss, confusion in an unidentifiable dimension. There I was, on the cold dirt floor and there was no waking up, no coming to or returning to what I had known my-*self* to be. I or the I, I called myself was no more. It felt so strange to even use this pronoun.

Nature or the natural process of my descent, I describe it as being tossed out, banned, banished from the familiar world. I became a displaced woman. A bag in the wind, seeking a root, a base, a home or even a familiar face. All I knew looked different, uncomfortably different. I was weakened physically, emotionally and spiritually. I was easy pray for the demons, as they came to finish me off.

I did have one compass that allowed me to breathe in all of this chaotic trauma, my faith and my purpose here on Earth. I realized warriors are born, not raised. I recognized my warrior spirit from early on. My heart's capacity to love is enormous. I fully recognize my soul to be a Light receiver and giver. I am pure love and I emit pure love.

I find it immensely difficult to accept what I have encountered on my journey thus far. The most devastating series of morbid losses, abuse, degradation, disrespect, violation of my whole being. All of this from the people I trusted and loved and thought loved me. It is a hard pill to swallow, betrayal. It is by far the hardest to forgive and to heal from in my opinion.

Let's go back to the beginning of time, my timeline as I recall. 1969 was a year of many wild world events. Man supposedly landed on the moon, the Mets, those lovable losers, won the World Series, and I was born!

I was almost aborted by my mom with a metal hangar. Thankfully she did not succeed. I protested I'm sure, or she gave up with the primitive style of mutilation. So funny how she chose to sit in a bathtub filled with water. It would hurt her more than me which was in my favor. My mom told me she was just upset with my father who felt she had tricked him into the pregnancy. Eventually they worked things out and I was born into the world on May 11. I could hardly wait, as cigarettes and Chinese food were a disastrous combination. I wanted out of that belly to breathe in some fresh air. To no one's surprise, I was born with asthma thanks to my chain-smoking giver of life. To top it off, I was a preemie baby weighing in at only 3.5 pounds.

I had to stay in the hospital two months before coming home. The journey of fighting for my life was set in motion. My DNA blueprint was set to Warrior Mode and I have been fighting ever since. I gained the proper weight and was sent to the place I would call home. I was placed in the care of my mom, the most important being in my evolution. I lost the battle of living in a luxury location with wealthy parents who spoke loving words and used kind gestures as their affirmations of love.

I would have loved to have supportive parents that encouraged me in seeking my dream and passions. My parents were definitely not that caliber, and unfortunately, I was molded by the trauma they inflicted upon me. I got the short stick and I knew it was going to be very challenging. I came into this world aware and awake to many things. I knew I had some kind of wild abilities, a powerful force within. I just did not know to what extremes I would be tested to know that they were real.

I wanted to recall it all and live it all. I came out of the birth canal, eager to live with zest and vigor. I wanted to experience everything I could with what I had been born into. I knew I was limited as being born in the armpit of New Jersey. Newark was certainly a beautiful city at one time. I just arrived a few decades too late to enjoy it. I came out in the worst time in Newark's history. Two years prior, the riots of 1967 altered our existence and our balance of life. A news clipping of what resulted of this tragic event, below summarized it well. No matter the color skin, we had to pick up the pieces and find a way to live together. There was little harmony or peace in this city and I was thrust into it. I had to absorb this unrest and hate in the air with fear overshadowing me. Thankfully, my heart led me. By the time I was ready to begin school, I was considered a minority. Our neighborhood was abandoned and a new one emerged from the ashes, unlike the Phoenix from Egyptian mythology, which was consumed in fire and rose again as a more beautiful bird, this was not the case.

"The turbulence also left an enduring legacy in molding perceptions of the city, even though those impressions vary widely. To some, the flames and violence were riots wrecking neighborhoods and driving away white and middle-class residents, feeding a notion that Newark was a dangerous and broken place. Or was it a rebellion, the uprising of a long-oppressed community that had finally had enough. From that, a new sense of empowerment was born."

This was a stark difference from when my grandfather, an Italian immigrant who walked the streets of Newark in the forties and fifties pushing a huge metal cart selling hot potatoes wrapped in tin foil for a nickel. He was given the name Ufumo or Smokey and was revered by many in the old ward. My grandfather was even depicted in a book about the lost city. They recalled the fond memories of smoke coming from his cart, and lines of children and adults waiting for a hot potato to warm their hands in depth of the freezing winters.

# MY FAMILY

My father, Carmine was born into wealth. His family owned an impressive portfolio of Real Estate. He was the type of man that was very quiet and did not show his anger or fears. He handled life with finesse. He even walked with finesse. I can say everything he did was with this sort of soft, gentle expression of energy. That is what I loved about him. I often felt bad for him having to endure my mom's rage and verbally abusive attacks. They would often fight over money issues, and it broke my heart. I declared on one of those tumultuous days that money was evil and I hated it. If only I had known I sealed my financial grave with that declaration, I would have taken it back.

I remember the exact moment I declared it, crouched down on the floor holding my ears crying. My wish was from my heart that broke each time they fought. I could not stand to hear them fight about money. I repeated over and over that I hated money.

I was daddy's little girl. I loved him so much. My dad was the apple of my eye and I would do anything to see him smile. I would wait all day and night for him to return home. He worked all day and on weekends he would go to the racetrack to bet on horses.

Since he was a very reserved man, it was difficult to be with him. He would not say much, but instead acted upon how he felt. He would nod his head to answer and spoke only when necessary. My love for him was so pure and at the age of two, I can actually remember him picking me up from my crib and carrying me around. The story my mom told me was he would pick me up and over his shoulder and I would reach out for her knickknacks that were shiny on a shelf. My dad would hold me, my face toward the shelf in the living room so I can reach them. I would grab each one, giggle, then throw it down, until each lay on the floor. The carpet caught the fall so nothing was damaged. It was our little ritual every night. I adored my father and loved him so much I created a negative belief for myself. It was one I had discovered during a healing meditation.

I had to undo this belief and be set free once and for all. I wanted to support my dad in any way. I knew money was an issue, so if we would go out to lunch, I would not order much to eat. I did not want to spend his money. I thought it would cause a huge fight. I created a belief that to show my love to men, I must not spend their money. I have been a cheap date far too long. Well, money has nothing to do with it. I showed my love by being considerate of other's money.

A disturbing fact is my dad would never hug me or my sisters. I would try to hug him and his hands would go up and he pet me on the head. I finally realized it was because of my mom's constant fear of sexual abuse. She was molested as a child and would often say to us, you better tell me if anyone touches you, even if it's your father. She would hammer this fear into us and it deteriorated our connection with him.

My mom, Geraldine – or Gerry – was born unto immigrant parents and was one of eight siblings. She was forced to drop out of eighth grade to support the family. She described her upbringing as a very sorrowful time. It was very difficult being so poor. She desperately wanted a different life. She told me how much she wanted to be singer, to just be someone in the world. Early on, she realized her survival would be her greatest endeavor in this life. Gerry began working and creating what she could with the little opportunities she had. The city was torn to pieces and the men off to war, very slim pickings as she described. At twenty-two she got pregnant with my older sister Selena. Her father was a Latin man who immediately left the picture.

She now was a single mom working at night to support her child.

It was difficult to find a career with no education to speak of, so she started bartending in the neighborhood sports bar. The Sports Rest was located on Garside Street, the street we lived on. It was convenient for her to work and have my grandmother watch Selena. One magical night, Carmine walked in the bar to have a scotch on the rocks. She locked eyes with him and the story of Geraldine and Carmine began.

My mom was proud to have him by her side. From what I was told, he loved her and would help her take care of my sister, who was two years old at the time. Carmine did make it clear to her that he did not want children or marriage, as he was thirty-five and set in his bachelor ways. He was a free bird, flying whenever and wherever he chose. He even had a beautiful little red convertible Fiat with white leather seats to match his bachelor lifestyle.

The car seats would later be mutilated with a steak knife by Gerry in a fit of jealous rage. The wrath of Gerry was undeniably the worse curse to endure. The ladies did love him as he was 6ft tall and very handsome.

One beautiful sunny day, he said let's go for a ride. I was so excited. I jumped in and closed the door. We are cruising and having such a fun time, all of a sudden, he made a sharp left turn and my hand gripped the armrest tightly. The next thing I knew, my door swung open and I was hanging out of the car looking at the ground.

I screamed so loudly, my dad immediately grabbed me by my pants and pulled me back into the car. It was definitely another close call for my little life. We had another close call a few years prior to this one. My dad would take me and my sister Selena to the park on the weekends while mom worked. I loved the swings and the sliding boards. My favorite was both of us on the swing and dad would push us both to try to go the highest. My sister, being older, could jump off the swing while at its apex.

On this sunny day, I was on the giant slide, it was so tall that when I looked down, I could see the top of my dad's head. I went up and down so many times, on the final one, I put my two hands on the one side and looked down at my dad to tell him to watch me and I immediately toppled to the ground. I fell about ten feet and smashed my head on the concrete. My mom went crazy when she saw me with a bloodied head. We got through that one with a lot of screaming, cursing, and drama.

My mom had a brass character who held nothing back, felt everything and was ignorant to whom she offended. My dad described her as a bull in a china shop. She spoke and misspoke so often, which foreshadowed the abusive episodes my sisters and I would endure. I knew even as a little child she was acting out her own turmoil of abuse and pain. She had such loving qualities that somehow redeemed her demonic side. Her soft spot was to help children and to give them what she did not have. We were never denied the things we needed or wanted.

Our clothes, our shoes and our hair were all taken care of meticulously. It was her deepest wish to give us what she never had as an immigrant child. She spoke of having to put newspapers on her feet because they did not have shoes to wear. The filth ring of dirt around her neck stained her clean clothes. They knew not much of cleanliness. I felt so badly and sad for her and it made me understand her current manic disorder. I did however realize it was detrimental to my health and emotional growth.

I had the sense to pray for strength to overcome this horrible reality. I wanted to come out unscathed or rather normal once done with childhood. An impossible endeavor that probably could never be accomplished. I had a long way to go and once the first event happened, I wanted to be released from this family at once.

The abuse by my mother became normal and a way of life. Today's standard, my mom would have been arrested and all of us would have been removed from the home. We knew it back then, yet we endured it. We loved her and feared her very much. I often wonder if someone reported her how would my life be right now. No regrets, just a wonderment of what would have been?

Forgiving her was easy, as she knew how to make up for her abuse and degradation. Shopping for toys and going to get ice cream. Ice cream is a nice reward after being physically and verbally abused. There were some fond memories and I wish I could recall them. It seems with time, age and mental overload memories faded in the wind. I recalled major events that surely changed my life and my path forever. Without her knowing, she drastically changed my trajectory in life. I still struggle with this knowledge.

What could I have been? What would I be doing today? Who would I be in the world? The answer is someone other than me. Love was part of my upbringing and I am forever grateful for whatever love was present. I do know I cultivated my own love and somehow rose above the inadequacies of my upbringing. I did become a very loving woman. I have deep compassion for life and I am always available to help my fellow brother or sister on this journey. I did experience wicked abuse, particularly two attacks that would mark my soul and alter my life's destiny forever.

## Selena

My sister Selena was born on March 10 1965, four years ahead of me. My father Carmine raised her and helped my mother care for her. I recall very little from our early ages. My first most favorite memories of my sister Selena were us dancing all the time. We would watch Danny Terrio and the dance moves he created on Saturday Night Fever movie with John Travolta. We copied all the moves. She would lead me in the hustle and the final move was always a lift up. She grabbed me under my shoulder and my knee and spun me around and around. It was so much fun to be connected to her. We hardly had any other interactions later in life as she had friends and she did not want me around. I would try to bust in on them but I would be shooed away. She hated me around her and her friends. One horrible day I recall us having a big fight on our front porch. I wanted to go with her and her friends and she said access denied.

I threatened to tell my mom she did something bad because mom would not hesitate to hit her. Selena was so angry about my threat she grabbed me and took all of my long hair and shoved it inside of my mouth.

It was easy because I was crying and I cried with my mouth open.

One equally traumatic moment for us both happened when I was just 5 years old. My mom was beating Selena up for something. I came out into the living room to find my mother dragging her by her hair on the ground. It reminded me of a cave man cartoon I had seen. As my mom is dragging her across the living room floor by her hair, she is also kicking her in stomach. I began to cry frantically and then became brave enough to shout "STOP MOM! LEAVE HER ALONE!", my mom turned toward me in all her rage and screams you want to be next? I quickly ran out of the room and hid in the closet. My gut, my heart and my head were spinning with fear. I wanted to save her from this horrible attack. I really did, but I could not. I was no match for this psychotic person. I felt powerless and to this day still feel it.

I have managed to overcome and reinstate my power on a daily basis. It is hard work to heal from traumatic experiences, but I am relentless and diligent to recover who I was meant to be.

In 1977 both Selena and I went into the hospital to have our tonsils removed. We had a nice room and our beds were side by side. I had just turned 8 years old. This memory was ingrained in my mind for several reasons. One night I was very bored and I went to use the bath room and saw a string hanging on the wall. It read, *Pull for Emergency.* I was so curious as to what would happen. I sneakily pulled it and suddenly loud alarms went ringing off. I ran back into my bed and put the covers over my head. In an instant 5 nurses came running in our room. They realized I pulled the string and told me to never do that again. I was so embarrassed but I truly did not know what I was doing or perhaps I truly wanted to know what it meant. Either way, I was reprimanded by mom as usual. I was spared a beating as I was recovering from surgery.

The other event that made this hospital stay memorable was on that very night my sister Selena was watching the TV hanging from the ceiling. I heard her crying so I looked over at her and she was sobbing uncontrollably.

I didn't know what made her so sad, then I saw on the news that Elvis Presley had died. Selena loved him as many of the teenage girls did. It was strange to witness her have emotions for someone she never met before.

As we got older, mom would appoint me Selena's chaperone. She was dating a guy named Sonny.

She would drive my mother's blue Buick to go on dates with him. I would be in the back seat while they made out on his porch. Sometimes they would leave me there for an hour. One night, I got bored and I hopped into the front seat of the car and drove off. I recall Sonny was running down the street screaming for me to stop. I kept going and drove all the way around the block. I was only thirteen years old. This began my early days of stealing my mom's car to pick up my friends and cruise around the city. I got so good at driving that she let me drive, as our neighborhood was getting dangerous to walk around. She preferred me driving than walking to meet friends. I was initially shocked but she saw my driving skills and was very impressed.

On the night before my big sweet-sixteen party, I got arrested for driving without a license. My mom came down the precinct with her Italian wooden spoon, she was preparing gravy(sauce) for the party. I thought she was going to hit me at first but she did not. She got me out of jail and they set a hearing for me. On the way home she told me to tell her everything that had happened. She made a point to tell her every detail and to not leave anything out. I explained that I was driving with Angela and Vincenza in Branch Brook Park and on a turn the car was making a funny noise. I had enough sense to pull over on the grass. I tried to start it, but it would not turn over. We sat there for a while and decided that Vincenza would go to a pay phone to call her boyfriend who was a tow truck driver. I am now sitting in in the car with Angela and waiting for her to get back. A police man parks behind us and comes to the window.

He asked me what are we doing here. I explained everything and he then asks for my driver's license. I had this as my plan if I ever got stopped and now, I had to use it. I pull out my sister's license and registration. The cop was going for it, yet at the last minute he asked "Do you always wear a different name on your neck"? I looked down and touched my gold name plate that said Violet all in diamonds and turned white. I stuttered and said "Well, not really". He then asked me to get out of the car and arrested me, putting me into the back seat of his squad car.

My mother said not to worry, I will figure it out and when we go to

14

court in a month, you will still get your driver's license. I was so upset and knew if I lost this case, I would not get my license until the age 21. Geraldine said she had a plan and it would work, and I believed her. The court date came and we were both in front of the judge. I had no idea what was up her sleeve, just hoped it would get me off the hook! Geraldine gets up in front of the judge and begins to tell the story of that day.

It began with us girls and an imaginary guy. A guy that was seeing my best friend, whom she was cheating on Angelo aka the tow truck driver. She went on to explain that the unnamed guy was driving her car. Your honor, when the car broke down the only solution was to call her boyfriend, Angelo, the tow truck driver, and the other boy had to disappear. My daughter jumped into the driver's seat to wait for Angelo. At this time the officer arrested my daughter for driving. The officer did not see my daughter driving the car, as it was turned off when he approached the vehicle. My daughter Violet was not driving and there are 2 witnesses to this. The judged looked at her with disdain, as he knew she had outsmarted him and the system. They did not have any proof I was actually driving.

When he banged the gavel, he looked so angry! Case dismissed! I saw my mom as a hero that day.

Geraldine was a smart woman even with all of her flaws, she loved us and wanted to see us flourish.

## Damiana

My sister Damiana was born on December 26, 1974. There was excitement throughout the house. My aunts were over and there was a lot of commotion. I was not that happy. I had 5 years of being the baby of the house. I was not ready to give up my attention. I tried to be happy for the new arrival but there was major resistance in my head. When she arrived, she did take all of my attention away. It was horrible at first, then I saw her as a good play mate. I loved playing with her and making her laugh.

There was this one time I was helping her walk and she lost balance and fell on the end table. She had cut her eyebrow open. My mom beat the living crap out of me. I was so shocked and it happened really fast. There was another time, I took her on a bike ride with me. Her little foot got caught in the wheel's spokes. I brought her home with a scraped ankle exposing bone and blood. I got beat up and chased all the way down the stairs into the street with a steak knife. I was eleven at the time and got really good at hook sliding. My mom was chasing me around cars, up and down the street. I hooked slide so much that she gave up. A hook slide was running in one direction so fast then doing an automatic stop and reversing your direction. I was the ultimate at it and it came in handy for this particular attack. What would she have done with that knife? I hid for hours, didn't come home until dark. She had calmed down and realized it wasn't that bad of an injury.

Damiana and I didn't have much in common since being five years apart. She was definitely the apple of my dad's eye. He loved her and would spend a lot of time with her. I was busy in school and working and did not have any quality time to spend with him. They would go to dinner and he would take her and her friends places. I was jealous that they spent time together but I had moved on and made a very busy life with friends and work responsibilities.

One memory that hurts me to this day, was the absence of my sister at my big college performance. I was part of the cast of *Hair* a play, directed by a New York Choreographer. I was excited to perform 4 nights at our outdoor amphitheater. All of the cast made the props and some of the clothes. It was a triumph for me to participating in such a creative endeavor. I practiced until 11 pm every night, even though tired from working full time and attending classes full time. My mom and my older sister Selena attended the first night. I looked around for Damiana but she was nowhere to be seen. She declined the invitation and did not attend any of the four-night engagement performances. I overlooked it at the time as her being busy or not caring about seeing a play. Later on, I realized that was a prelude to how she would disrespect me in much harsher ways. I have forgiven her actions towards me.

# TWISTED BY TRAUMA: HOLLYWOOD IS FOR WHORES

As I mentioned, my dad was my everything and I wanted to impress him. I would always prepare a dance when he returned home in the evening. I would put on his favorite albums; Burt Bacharach, Perry Como and others of that genre. I would practice a twirly dance over and over until I felt it was perfect for performing. This one evening was so exciting because I had prepared a doozy. A few twirls, two summersaults and a half split. Anxiously I awaited to hear him enter the kitchen door. I had the records all set to play. I was a great choreographer and director, and it would be a perfect performance by me. Finally, he entered the living room with his scotch on the rocks and he sat in his favorite chair.

I peeked out of my room and said to my dad, "I have a surprise for you". I asked him to tell me when he was ready. I ran in put the needle down on the record and retreated behind stage, as soon as the song began, I made my entrance! My long pink gown flowed as I burst into my twirls singing loudly, I am going to be a star and two summersaults a couple more twirls and my finale, I said. "You will see dad, I am going to go to Hollywood, I am going to be a star!" My arms were spread as wide as heaven and in my half split, I was in all my glory, feeling invincible.

In an instant, I heard the heavy pounding of footsteps coming in from the kitchen.

I looked up with a coy smile and all of a sudden, I am being attacked by my mother. She grabbed both of my arms that were raised up in a victory position, forced them down to my sides and squeezed them with her long nails digging in while lifting me up. She screamed in my face. "*Hollywood*? Hollywood is for whores! You must want to get fucked?" My little six-year-old heart pounded out of my chest. I couldn't breathe from her energy and the pure embarrassment she caused in front of my love, my daddy. I looked at him at glance and I felt all my power drain from me. My innocence spilled onto the floor like piss running down my leg. I do not know if I peed but it sure felt like I had lost control of all of my bodily functions. She continued with asking me if I wanted to get fucked on the couch? I had no idea what she meant, but I understood sex was a very bad word and whatever came with it. She, later in life, apologized by explaining she heard the stories of the casting couch. I understood and it came all out with the recent #metoo movement. Putting it bluntly, Hollywood was a cesspool of sexual predators.

My little 6 year old soul froze in shock at that moment, to never feel safe again in my home or in life. I was so disturbed and hurt and filled with deep sadness. I was so deeply embarrassed and full of shame in front of my daddy. I only wanted to be his little princess and now I was something else. I was bad, a whore or not good anymore. All of this running through my little mind was too much. Only later in my life would I discover my mother's fears were prophetic.

I ran to my room and grabbed my mom's makeup suitcase and began filling it with my pajamas, onesies and a few Barbie dolls. I walked out of the house down the 3 flights of stairs to reach a dark and lonely hallway. I flew open the screen door to look out into the desolate streets. In front of me, an empty parking lot that belonged to an Italian Restaurant and nothing but broken glass and the downtrodden streets of Newark to walk upon.

I realized at that moment, I had to go back and live like a prisoner in this place I called home. I wanted to disappear and leave to a faraway place and never return. I guess I wanted to go to Hollywood, a one-way ticket would have been great. Being anywhere else would have been better than to go back up there to an insufferable existence. I could not be me or be who I wanted. I did not understand what this was all about but I knew it meant one thing, I was not able to express myself safely. I would do my best to make this work. I turned around and looked up the dark stair case and I realized no one had come for me. I felt so hurt.

Was I not good enough to come after? Was I a whore who was no good to anyone? Did my mom even love me? After all, she had tried to abort me. All of these beliefs were twirling in my head, instead of my dance moves. I now had to process this load of crap. I began crying, a cry so deep, from my sorrowful soul. Each step I took, to rise up into the hell I just ran from caused me to cry more. Slow and dreadful steps, up three long flights and all I could think of is what kind of life will I have? I didn't deserve this rude awakening. The ripping to pieces of my innocent dream. I wanted and needed love, compassion and support for my dreams.

Fat chance. If I knew there would have been more abuse, I would have run away that night. The strangest occurrence as I got to the top step, I sensed someone. I could not see anything and all of a sudden, my dad stepped out of the darkness and reached down to pick me up. I was so delighted, so relieved he looked for me. He was there all along hearing me cry as I walked up.

I jumped in his arms and he held me tightly. I cried so much. He told me. "Don't listen to your mother. She is a nut job and everything will be okay." He did make me feel better but my soul was definitely damaged. I felt as though I was frozen in that moment. I was never quite the same and my disdain for mother was growing. I had to tolerate her and abide by her but inside me I was rebelling. I know my father was just tolerating her madness also.

The fighting was so bad at times it was dangerous to be around. One time she was so angry she threw a large, three-foot-tall porcelain statue of a flamenco dancer holding a violin out of our third-floor window. It shattered into a million tiny shards. Thankfully no one was hurt or killed.

Only once did it escalate to physical violence as my father was not the abusive type of man. They were fighting in the living room and she was so out of control my dad grabbed her wrist to subdue her and she fell backwards and hit her back on the faux fire place. All hell broke loose yet once again, but we survived. There was a funny light to all of this chaos. My dad would often call her a garbage can during their fights, with a garbage mouth. He was not used to this crass behavior.

He never cursed or spoke ill of anyone. He was a true gentleman. My mom grew tired of him calling her a garbage can and never had a come- back. One day during their usual fighting session, she got him to the angry point where he would say, you know, Geraldine, you are a garbage can with a garbage mouth! She burst out with a cheeky retort. "Oh yeah? Well, you're my lid!" They both started laughing and it became part of the Galletto folklore. To this day it is remembered as Gerry's greatest come-back!

# NIGGER LOVER

It was a normal summer morning and mama Geraldine would delight in her 3 cups of coffee, smoking her cigarettes while gossiping with our African American friend and neighbor Gwen. I was always so full of energy, vibe, and gusto. My soul was on fire and it always sought adventure, creativity and fun. I was eight years old and I still had the desire to create and express myself. Napoleon was Gwen's son. He was the youngest of the five siblings. His mom dragged him to her gossip session and I was delighted to have a friend or anyone to entertain. The television was always on in the background and today it was tuned to *Days of Our Lives*. I was watching it and intrigued by the actor's movements and how their words matched perfectly. I was so hyped on reproducing this scene I just watched. I thought Napoleon would be the perfect supporting character.

The scene was so simple, a wife by the stove cooking a meal with a big smile on her face, all of a sudden, she heard the front door close and from the other room, her husband yelled. "Honey I'm home!". She quickly wiped her hands on her apron, removed it and ran into the foyer to greet her loving husband. His arms were opened wide as she flew into them, he then picked her up and began to spin her around planting a kiss on her cheek. I adored this scene and wanted to recreate it. I had my actor right next to me. I asked him if he wanted to act and he said yes.

I went into director mode and told him I would be in the other room and I gave him his lines and I said on the count of three etc.

I really loved being a director, this love would soon be mine. "One! Two! Three! Action!" Napoleon said the magic words, I came running in to greet him, he picked me up and spun me around and we both fell to the ground! The noise from the fall was so loud and obnoxious that both of our moms came running. They found us laughing and rolling around on the green shagged carpet. My mother went into hysterical mode and reached down pulling me up by my hair. She screamed. "You nigger lover! What are you doing?"

She began punching me with her one hand and pulling me up by my hair with the other. A fun magical creative moment turned into the second most horrifying embarrassing abusive moment of my little life. It was all I could stand. I was so embarrassed once again. She called Gwen's son a nigger. I was completely and devastatingly shocked into shame again. Gwen was so upset she yelled at my mother and told her to never speak to her again. From that day on, we had to live an uncomfortable existence. I ignored Napoleon as if he didn't exist. I was so ashamed of what I did, what trauma I caused him. I still have not fully reconciled this event. I remember feeling so awkward for a very long time. When we finally moved, it was so liberating. This life of mine had started out so badly, so what else could happen? I had to fight through, rise up, and become the woman I was destined to be.

Living out the rest of my youth in this environment was horrible, yet I made it work. God had given me a solid soul connection to him. I can only describe it as a warrior spirit. I would always be fighting something invisible inside and had to tolerate the outside oppression. I had extreme faith due to this strong knowing/connection to a source unseen. It gave me rest, peace, and strength to carry on. The fight for my soul was ever present, looking back in my journals, I was under attack by an invisible force often.

Thankfully my mom enrolled me in Catholic School. I contribute this to my deepened faith. I attended St. Francis Xavier Grammar School and Our Lady of Good Counsel High School. I have such great memories of those days. I understood the energy of Jesus Christ and it felt so good to be in that presence.

I loved to sing in the choir. I always felt protected and loved during those times. My sense of compassion for others grew and I knew my calling was to be a teacher due to my love for children and learning.

I began to look back into my childhood writings. I had been journaling since I was eleven. I loved writing and documenting my life as it was happening all from my perspective. I mostly wrote to keep track of the strange experiences not only my daily life. I wrote about having disturbingly lucid dreams. One night, there was a voice screaming in my ears. It grew louder into a growling laughter that mocked me, chased me. The evil laugher taunting me said, "You can't run from me!" I was grasping for air, heart beating as I tried to get away. I woke up hitting my wall terrified and was sure there was a real person coming after me to kill me.

I recalled another dream where I was laying on my left side and I was awoken by a presence in my bed, a fuzzy vibration overtook my whole body. I was being restrained and seduced. I forced myself awake fighting to remove this energy and when I opened my eyes, two ghosts were at the foot of my bed. They were staring at my mirrored closet doors. The man was dressed in an army uniform and the woman in a 1950's floral dress with round collar. I was frozen in fear and quickly closed my eyes asking God to make them go away. I repeated it over and over and squinted my one eye but they were still there. It was all just a dream, right? All of these memories were just clues of confirmation that I had been in pursuit by the dark spirit world. I recalled the earliest of my attacks was when I was five years old. I would endure many disturbing sexual dreams as well. I did not know what these dreams represented.

It was as if someone in my mind wanted to have these recurring dreams. I was walking through a well-groomed garden, down a grassy path with huge green, forty-foot pine hedges in the dark of night in a white gown not knowing where I was going. I was innocently walking and suddenly the ground opened up and I slipped through a secret underground passage. I fell all the way down into a dungeon of sorts. I recalled screaming all the way down.

I then found myself as an adult in a sexual dungeon with naked men and women. From innocence to immorality in a quick flash. I would struggle to wake, praying to God or Jesus to help me wake up. I did not like this dungeon, the smell, the energy, the darkness. I begged to be removed. I eventually woke up after praying so hard. I thanked God and drifted back to sleep. That exact dream would reoccur several more times, until I demanded to be left alone. I absolutely demanded to never go back there and with that declaration, I never had that dream ever again. I chalked these all up to just weird occurrences. I never told a soul about the sexual dreams as I did not want to put to words what I saw down in the dungeon.

My teenage years were much better. I had many friends and loved school. I excelled in all areas. Looking back at this time seems so magical. I had a crush on Vinny. He was my first real love at thirteen. Once night my doorbell rang, I ran down the stair case to see who it was and Vinny was there with his hands behind his back. I opened the screen door and said hello! His beautiful big brown eyes and smile twinkled with joy as he handed me the most perfect stuffed animal. I blushed and coyly smiled as I leaned in for a thank you kiss. We were in love, and, of course, I ruined it. I recalled this warm summer day when Vinny and I met in between our houses. I lived on Tenth Street, and he lived on Ninth Street. The sun shone so bright. The tree leaves were glistening and birds were singing. We walked hand in hand laughing. Love was beaming off of our hearts, colliding with the atmosphere.

We turned toward each other, holding both hands and we begin to spin around and around. All the while, beaming smiles, eyes locked in love. We spun, much like Jack and Rose did in *Titanic* when he showed her the love of life the steerage passengers enjoyed. We spun into dizziness, and out of my wretched mouth came the words. "I hope you know; nothing lasts forever!"

Those words were spoken as a defense mechanism against being hurt by love. I shattered the beautiful moment into tiny shards of glass.

Vinny's face distorted with pain. I broke his heart. My heart shrivels every time I recall what I did. I basically stopped our fledgling love, for fear it would end. I had a macabre perception of life and this was just the beginning.

# HIGH SCHOOL DAYS

Our lady of Good Counsel HS was originally an all-girl's school. The year I enrolled it became co-ed. It was a quaint school building with a beautiful church. Since we were a small high school, we were all close and I recalled it felt like family. Among the students and staff there was always love and respect present. I had many friends who made the whole experience fun.

One friend I really bonded with and felt as though we could have been twins separated at birth. Angela was my ride or die! We laughed so much and had the most amazing adventures. We even were a little devious. One morning, as we walked to the bus stop, we decided we didn't want to go to school. The bus for *Bloomfield Center* stopped in front and she grabbed my hand and we climbed aboard. *Bloomfield Center* was the best for shopping and eating.

Once on the bus, I said. "We are going to have to come up with a good lie or else we are going to be in big trouble."

Angela came up with the craziest idea. She said, "Let's say that as we were waiting for the bus, and someone came up to me and stole my gold chain off of my neck!"

I was in shock but it sounded plausible as we did live in Newark, the crime capital of New Jersey. I said, "I will scratch your neck to make it look real." I recalled dragging my nails down her neck and her screaming. We went shopping, ate pizza at our favorite place, and even went to the park. It was an amazing day. I guess our teenage mentality was working overtime thinking we could get away with our scheme. I will report that we were never exposed. We kept the lie a secret till this day, now for all to read, see truth will always be revealed.

The nuns were wonderful except for a few meanies. If Sister Elizabeth, the disciplinary nun, found this out, we would both be expelled with signs on our back that read *Truants*! I recall this one horrible day, I was in class and I saw through the glass door that Sister Elizabeth was pointing at me, and curling her finger towards her. I looked around to see if it was indeed me, she was signaling. My eyes opened wide and my heart sank, as it was me that she wanted. My mind could not fathom why would the disciplinary nun would want to speak with me. I did nothing wrong. Did she find out about the fake heist? My heart was pounding out of my cardigan sweater and my saddle shoes were tapping the floor. Sweat from anxiety began to form around my neck.

To describe her in one word, frightening. Her stature: wide and tall, she had shoulders 3 feet wide and piercing blue eyes. Her mean voice and demeanor were intimidating. She never did show any liking to me or my friends. I was called a truant by her many times. I tried to steer clear of this nun. I got up from my desk and slinked across the classroom floor. She gave me an ice-cold stare and said, "Follow me." I followed her to the main office and she asked me if I had a brush.

I said, "Yes, in my bag." I handed it to her. She roughly turned me around and began brushing and pulling my curly locks. The brush would not go through as my curls were tussled. I screamed for her to stop.

Her exact comment was. "Why don't you brush your hair? All the others girls have long beautiful brushed hair!"

I asked her to stop pulling my hair and asked if I could call my mother. I told her most of the girls in school were Latinas and had straight hair. I let my mom explain to her and she did. My mom requested she leave me and my hair alone. I made it through the rest of my time at OLGC free of drama.

The only drama I encountered was the play I was asked to join.

My teacher, Mr. Gomes, was head of the drama department, as well as our history teacher. He asked me to audition for the lead female role of Rachel, in the play *Inherit the Wind*. I was shocked he had asked me, and deep inside feared coming close to my once forgotten dream. My mother's face screaming at me, calling me a whore, was always there. I told him. "No thanks I don't think I can do that." I have to admit, when he asked me, I was thrilled to think about me being on stage acting. My fear was too great and my esteem was too low to even see it as a reality.

Mr. Gomes did not stop at no. A week later he asked me again and actually pleaded with me just to audition. He listed all of my friends who were already involved. I somehow felt his belief in me and decided to audition. He was so excited and that was enough for me. I got the part, picked up the script, and learned all my lines. Participating in this production was so much fun. I discovered that I could act! I felt a new sense of freedom and a huge shift in my being. I believe Mr. Gomes' persistence was just what I needed to heal my early trauma. God works wonders through people. Of course, the next year when he asked me to try out for that years' play again, and be a true co-lead. It was called *Flowers for Algernon*, but I stood firm and turned him down. I learned this much later, but he was disappointed at the chance he would not direct me again.

# TWENTY-YEAR-OLD VIRGIN

I finally manifested my true love in 1989. Meeting Ronnie was one of the best things in my life. I declared I wanted to wait until I found my true love to give virginity to. One ominous night, I went out dancing with my friends to Joeys Nightclub. While standing on line to get in, I met this handsome guy. I was 20 years old and he was 27. I had been praying for God to send me my husband every day. I would cry and complain often to my friends. They would say, "Don't wait for Mr. Perfect, just do it!" I had my heart set on the most romantic, beautiful and perfect experience. I wanted true love and connection, not just sex. Once we were inside the club, he bought me a drink and we were talking non-stop. He had the bluest eyes and such a beautiful smile. I was smitten to say the least. We danced all night, laughing and connecting soul to soul.

Our love story began and I thanked God for this beautiful gift. We were inseparable and I was sure he was the one. On our special night he created the most romantic setting taking me to dinner then after had lit candles, flowers and music. I will always remember that night and I knew my patience was worth every day I cried and prayed for my one true love to come. God had his own timing and if you allow him, he will deliver your truest desires.

We were engaged after six amazing months together. We had the type of love that was in storybooks. Whenever we went out to eat or at home, we sat next to each other. We had to always be touching skin to skin. Our intimacy was through the roof. I never knew how incredible our love making was until long after we broke up. We would make love for hours and hours not stop. He would try to explain how rare it was for a couple to orgasm many times in one evening, but as a virgin I never could understand. I did not have any reference. He once explained all of his friends and their girlfriends had sex once or twice a week. I would stare at him as if he were speaking Chinese. I just knew we were magnetic and destined to be together. In my heart, I would always desire him and cherish our love. I was happy to have a life partner and was determined not to ruin it.

One particular day, we went to eat at a Japanese restaurant. It was the type that you sit around with strangers and the chef cooked you an individual dish. It was so fun – or so I thought. The next thing I knew Ronnie stood up and cursed at the girl and the guys across the way. He abruptly said. "Let's go, we are leaving." I was so shocked and dismayed. I protested because I had no clue as to what could have happened. I was oblivious.

As we left the restaurant, he dragged me out and we got in his car, he began to explain. Ronnie was at the salad bar and the girl who had been across from us went up to Ronnie and grabbed his butt. She made a sly pass at him, and the table she began to flirt and ultimately was disrespecting me. That is when he stood up and called her a Bitch. I was in shock to know all this happened right in front of me. I quickly was informed how the world worked.

I was a bit too innocent when it came to aggressive women. He was definitely a very handsome man and I knew there would be more. There was another time when Ronnie was out playing pool with his friends and a woman approached him. She asked him. "Hey do you have a girlfriend?"

He replied. "Yes, I do."

She began to flirt with him anyway, and said, "Well, she is not here."

He turned to her and said yes, she is. She asked where? He touched his heart and said she is right here! The woman walked away with her tail between her legs. I loved this story, and although I was not there, I do believe it happened, as Ronnie wrote me the most beautiful poems. He did the most kind and romantic things. It was such a perfect love story.

Unfortunately, this would not be a happy ever after. In fact, it was over after two years. I was so heartbroken and wondered why this had to happen. I felt betrayed by God and by Ronnie. There had been a song released by Don Henley about a year earlier called *The End of the Innocence.* There was a line from the song that broke my heart. "When happily ever after fails, and we've been poisoned by these fairy tales."

Ronnie had requested I drop out of college and to stop hanging out with my friends. He would take care of me and we were one against the world. I did not understand this type of mentality. I was raised to be independent and college was already ingrained in mind. I loved college and learning. My dream of becoming a teacher or biologist was at stake. I loved him unconditionally, or so I thought. I knew I would not be happy with this glum description of our future. I would have to make the most difficult decision and call off our engagement. I gave him back the beautiful ring. I cried for a very long time. I read books on how to cope with heartbreak.

I dove into my studies and joined the players club. I even auditioned for the famous play *Hair.* I got the part of dancer in the entourage. It was such an amazing experience. This breakup taught me, just because you love someone, does not mean they are good for you. It was a hurtful lesson to learn but it helped me later in life. I thanked God for the beautiful gift and began to heal my heart.

Trying to pick up the pieces of me. I began to realize the magnitude of damage that was done to my psyche. I endured devastating hits to my innocent little one. My future life and destiny felt frozen in time. Trauma had damaged me and my relationships. I really could never figure it out or know how to fix it. I sought out so many avenues of healing and self-empowerment.

I partook in the Landmark Forum, a worldwide seminar that revealed to you the truth of your existence. The strong suits held your façade together. It is all a façade. To.be on this Earth is a game of charades and you must play. One must plug into the system and then try to find a frequency where you can maneuver. The beauty is you can slip in and out of other frequencies, aka, realities. It is an amusing place to navigate through.

I have come to understand there are no mistakes here on Earth, so all is pre-planned. Although I never understood it at the time, I first learned this concept in high school from Mr. Gomes in our *World Cultures* class. There was a French priest named John Calvin, who believed in predestination. In essence, your life had already been laid out before you. I did hypnotherapy to try to undo the shame and shock my system was carrying. I became a Reiki healer and certified STT practitioner, which stands for Spontaneous Transformation Technique created by the celebrated healer Jennifer Mclean I was also initiated in the Light and Sound mediation.

I became a vegetarian at this time to reach enlightenment. I am now Vegan, championing for the rights of animals. I was initiated in to Krishna and Buddhist religions. I wanted to learn and seek out the truths of those who came before me. I read hundreds of books on healing and philosophies of the greats. I immersed my soul into a purposeful healing journey. I was so determined to clear my slate so I could live the life of my dreams. During all of this I still encountered more drama and abuse.

My awareness that DNA stores trauma, led me to understand I may never fully heal my little one. I can pacify her and console her but never fully recover her light and innocence. Writing this is my attempt to reach my inner self deep inside. I wanted her to come out and be herself. Living a shadow self has been very painful. A constant nagging feeling like you are wrong, your path, your soul, your journey all not real even if it is.

My life's purpose twisted by trauma. Even if your life looks as though you are accomplishing things and doing great things, the feelings inside do not match. This is the great contrast all humans experience. I can only say enough, that my faith in a power greater than myself kept me seeking the truth. I became obsessed with knowing thyself.

My beloved father passed away in 1993. I recalled being in the hospital seeing him in his bed. I felt powerless. I was shocked to see my shining armor scared for his life. One winter night, he came home from the race track at around eleven PM. He walked up the twelve icy, brick steps to the front door. He pulled open the screen door and he lost his balance. At 5 AM, my mom went outside to see if his car was there and she found him at the bottom of the step unconscious. There was a pool of blood staining the snow by his head. She called 911 and rushed him to ER.

We all went to the hospital the next day. He seemed to be perfectly fine. He had a minor concussion. They ran all tests and x-rays to make sure he did not break any bones. The news we never saw coming was he had Oat Cell cancer of the lungs. The x-rays showed his lungs were cancerous. The doctor told my mother he did not have much time. I was not told directly but looking at my mother's state of being was enough.

I understood this was not going to end well. My most treasured moment with him was when I gave him massage on his neck. I used to give him feet massages when I was little. I remember him sitting on the edge of the couch and I would put my feet in the air and kick him with my little heels. It was so much fun. I got to massage him for the last time. Sitting and watching him deteriorate was very difficult. I saw his ego was hurt because he did not want us to see him this way. One day during my visit I was inspired to write a poem. It came out as if it was from y dads' perspective.

## CAN I GO HOME?

It's early in the morning and I'm on my way home
I don't want to go there, but when I get there, I want to stay
It's morbid and cold
Halls of pain-you forget your name
It's where the needle takes over your vein
You exist to pacify the ones who love you
Wish you had control to find someplace new
You hear voices but no one is there
You're like a flower suspended in air

Why do I have to stay here and the others leave
Is it because you believe that I will return to who I was before
Oh, can't you see, I can't be him anymore
The clock is ticking yet I lay still
I'll keep taking all these pills
To prolong a destiny that needs to be fulfilled
Is it time yet can I go home?
So, I can see my name in stone.
for my father, Carmine
My dad went home on December 3, 1993.

I was devastated because it happened so suddenly, in a span of just two months. I felt I did not have enough time to tell him how much I loved him. I always thought I would have the time. With him gone, I felt a sudden need to leave New Jersey. I was living with my younger sister in our first-floor apartment. She was constantly degrading and attacking me for trivial things. I would leave my apartment at eight AM and not return home until eleven PM. I had a full schedule, work, school, rehearsals etc. I would get home and she would yell at me for leaving a bagel dish in the sink. It began to wear on me and I just could not deal with her disrespect. All of the past issues with my mom came to light, and I realized my dad was the only person keeping me here.

I was seeking freedom from oppression. I wanted to be celebrated and all I received was disdain. The opportunity to move presented itself and I took it. My best friend had moved to Miami and invited me to come for an extended stay. I had planned to visit Miami after graduation from Montclair State University. I arrived in Miami on January 25, 1995. I never returned to New Jersey, except for holidays. I asked my dad for a sign to let me know if this is the best move for me. The next day, I went to get my car cleaned and I on the passenger floor board was a beautiful butterfly sitting there. It had flew into my can and died there. It was iridescent blue and in perfect condition. Butterflies signify freedom and transformation. I need both. I kept that butterfly in a little box as I drove all the way to Miami.

I was thrilled with my newfound freedom and independence. I

rented a home in South Miami with my friends from New Jersey. We had the most amazing times together. This was short lived, as one friend got pregnant and moved out. I desired to be in South Beach, as I was driving an hour to get to work. I needed to move again.

# TWIN FLAME

This experience was the most beautiful, intense and surreal. I was invited to my teacher friend's bachelorette party. It was on a cruise ship. It left from Fort Lauderdale and cruised into the open ocean. I will try to explain this but no words can give this justice or true description. We all were walking single file through a corridor, I believe I was the last one and as I came to the open area, I look up to see which way the girls went. I instantly locked eyes with this guy and fell into a deep freeze.

I could not move for what felt like five minutes. I described it as, my soul was ripped out of body and connected with his soul. They did a dancing "meet and greet", then it returned to me. I unfroze and looked around dazed and confused, feeling as though something happened. I moved my legs forward and had a realization this guy would be right behind me. I was so sure of it, and I was never surer of anything. I mean, I knew he was right behind me.

I began walking up the stairs to the upper deck. I dared to look behind me, and he was on the step below. I quickly turned forward; my heart was beating so fast. As soon as I reached the dance floor, his hand came toward me and I looked into his eyes again and felt a beautiful, loving energy cover me. He said hello I am Yohvanni. I knew him and he knew me. We held hands and danced deep into the night. We took a break and went to the top deck to look at the waning crescent moon that was high in the sky. He held me in his arms as if we had been long time lovers and watched as the approaching dawn barely lit the eastern sky. The familiar touch, the familiar soul, this was pure magical bliss. It was as if our souls were running the show.

I thought he was the most handsome man I had ever met. The funny thing is, we looked so alike. He was on vacation from Switzerland with his friends on the cruise. We both fell in love that night under the moon and stars. I cried when I found out he would be leaving back to Switzerland. I could not bear another heartbreak. I felt our love was real and it would somehow be all right. Then I found that he had a girlfriend back home. I could not help but get angry at God, feeling betrayed again. I now have discovered a pattern of heartbreaks.

He confessed he did not love her the way she deserved. He said he loved her like a sister and wanted to break up with her. I told him I would not speak to him until that happened. I was glad he lived far away, for this would have been hard to resist him. He called me often to check in and chat. It was nice to hear from him as we had so much in common.

One day he called and told me he had broken up with her. He was now planning to come to Miami. I was so ecstatic when I heard the news. My heart was filled up with hope and love. I would have to wait until February of 1997, a year from our first encounter.

We looked alike but people would seriously ask if we were brother and sister. We had the same green eyes, almond shape and our hair color, height, cheek bones. It was uncanny.

Months after my awakening ordeal, Yohvanni finally made the move to Miami. My friend Giordana allowed him to move into my room and we paid her more rent. After a few months, we wanted to get our own place. Yohvanni searched for our perfect home every chance he had. Yohvanni called me so excited because he had found the most perfect place for us to live.

I was so ecstatic too! He described it as a perfect place for lovebirds. It was a cute one-bedroom apartment that sat next to a canal. It was right next to St. Patrick's Cathedral and walking distance to the ocean. We were so happy and in love. We made this place a warm and loving home. I lost contact with Giordana after moving out when we had a minor falling out.

Life was moving fast, working and discovering the responsibilities of a relationship. I was ready to try to love again and make it work. Everything was blissful for a good eight months. I got him a chef position at the famous *Living Room Restaurant and Club*. Yohvanni struggled to process this crazy atmosphere.

He was immersed in so much stimulation, a stark difference from Switzerland. Most people could not handle the hyper stimulation. Drugs were always a high-risk endeavor that were the downfall of many people from small towns. I noticed a changed in his behavior. He would have to work late nights until five AM. I came and met him at the club. Later I found he was taking cocaine to stay awake. I knew he smoked weed, but this news broke my heart. His energy and demeanor changed and I confronted him.

I was not into drugs and did not approve. It began to separate us. He was enjoying the lifestyle too much. Fighting between us grew and after two years we broke up. It would take a toll on my physical body. I refused to eat for almost ten days. I got down to 125 pounds. I looked like a skeleton and felt like one too. My heart was torn into pieces. I felt as though my soul was missing. I could not function, and if it weren't for my students, I do not know how I would have continued.

I had to get up each day to teach my students. They depended on me and they were all I had to live for. I loved them so much and was grateful to have been their teacher. I wrote in my journal to stay sane. I tried to decode why love had been so horrible to me? What did I do to deserve this? I began reading about spirituality. I felt I needed some answers as to why I kept being ripped apart. My mind wanted solace, and I was going to seek until I found it.

I was initiated into Light and Sound Meditation. I read books all the New Age Books. I actually found out about Twin Flame Encounters. It explained everything I had just experienced with Yohvanni.

Our love story had cracked at the seams. I began to put my guard up and we started to slip away from each other. I found a letter from his ex-girlfriend from Switzerland, Jeannette. It was in German, so I brought it to Giordana to see if she could translate it for me. She basically said Jeannette was a doormat.

I said, "What?"

She couldn't even put it into English the words to describe what she wrote. Giordana said Jeannette gave her life up for him. She said that Jeanette declared that he was her breath, her soul, and her reason to live. I cried for hours when I heard this. I sat in the dark and thought about how much a person could love another.

I had never known this kind of love. I would give up and give in before I would love someone like this. I had pride and self-worth. As I thought deeper, I tried to fathom loving him like this, but I could not. I would be able to breath and to live without him. For this reason, I broke up with him and requested he go back to Switzerland to be with her. I wondered if my fear of pain would allow me to love like this one day. I saw Jeannette at first as a fool, but later I realized how brave she was to express her deepest feelings.

They are married with two beautiful children. The universe brought Yohvanni into my field once. In 2011, I was living in New Jersey and New York while my mom was ill. I got licensed as a commercial agent and working in the Upper Westside. I did photography gigs as well. I was in Penn station with all of my camera gear around my neck. I paced back and forth waiting for the train. Finally, it came and I jumped onto the mid-town. I stayed with my friend Chantelle when I worked late instead of traveling all the way to New Jersey.

When I got home, I opened up my laptop and there was a message on AOL from George, a mutual friend of Yohvanni and me. I had not spoken to him for so long and was pleasantly surprised. His message read. "Were you in Penn Station today with camera around your neck?"

I exclaimed. "Yes. Did you see me?"

He said it wasn't him, it was Yohvanni. My heart stood still and a wave of sadness came over me. I had not heard his name in over almost fifteen years. He said he saw me on the other side of the tracks and was calling my name, but I didn't hear him. I didn't hear him, and I knew the reason. God closed that portal, or connection, for me. Yohvanni was able to see me for he had still a desire for our love. I believe I blocked him to keep him faithful to his wife.

# SOUTH BEACH IN THE 90'S

I met Giordana, a beautiful hopeful girl, while we both bartending at the famous Italian Restaurant on South Beach called *Mezzanotte*. She and I had come from different walks of life but somehow South Beach brought us together. She left Germany to come to the United States for the American Dream. I guess I came for the same reason. I think it was more for my personal freedom.

South Beach brought everyone together for many reasons. The most beautiful part of living in South Beach was the diversity. I only knew of three races living in New Jersey. White (Italian), Black, and Spanish. That was all that surrounded us. It was refreshing to be immersed and in contact with other cultures.

Giordana, an only child, was from Manheim, Germany. She was the first authentic German I had met in my life. Luckily for her, her mother had purchased her a beautiful condo to live in on Millionaires Row at the famous *Seacoast Towers*. We became instant friends and our friendship was unique. I needed to move from Kendall to Miami Beach so I rented Giordana's second bedroom at the *Seacoast Towers*. I always dreamed of living on the ocean and now I was living it! I was the happiest I have ever been in my entire life. I shared with her that I met the love of my life and he was in Switzerland. I told her I am hoping he can visit Miami soon.

Giordana taught me so many new things. I began learning how to run to build stamina. We would run three times or more a week on the Ocean for forty-five minutes. The first time she encouraged me to run, I ran a few steps and collapsed. "New Jersey girls do not run!", I shouted. She persisted and acted like a running coach. It took me a while, but I got up to her speed and endurance. The first time I got the runners high, I was addicted. She never had to coerce me again.

I taught her how to cook Italian style. I also coached her on how to be less vulnerable. I had been trained to keep a hard exterior and hide my vulnerability. She was the complete opposite. We were perfect for teaching each other what we never were taught. We had so many dinner parties and frequented all the hot Spots. Memories of dancing all night surrounded by friends and the lights of South Beach are ingrained in my mind forever.

One beautiful memory was when my mom, who never flew in her life, came down to see me. She came down to help me buy me a car. I felt so much love from her and this act was so pure on her part. She wanted me to succeed and I truly forgave her for what she had done to me in my early years. We took her to dinner on Ocean and watched the sunset from our balcony after with a glass of champagne.

We celebrated her first time flying. The next day my mom and I went to the car dealership and I got my New SUV. I was so excited. I thanked *God* every second for this new reality. She enjoyed her time so much.

One Miami tragedy that stained my mind was when Gianni Versace was murdered. It was an eerie night on my way home to the *Seacoast Towers*. Traffic was backed up for miles. I just wanted to get home and eat. I had no idea what had happened as I was teaching a nine-hour day. I got rerouted and finally called Giordana to see what had happened. The houseboat that Andrew Cunanan barricaded himself in and later committed suicide was directly across from *Seacoast Towers*. No one could get through so I stayed at a friend's house for the night.

Since Miami was the most sought-after place to live in the 90s, one never knew who you could meet. *Mezzanotte* had lines wrapped around the corner to get in, most reservations were made two months in advance. Money, wine, music and dance on tap! The most prestigious people were patrons here.

I met Jack Nicholson, Al Pacino, Madonna, Mickey Rourke, Joe DiMaggio, Eddie Vedder, Don Johnson and Phillip Michael Thomas (Crocket and Tubbs) and so many other famous people while living and working in South beach. It was an amazing time to be alive in a place that had so much energy and money flowing through the streets. I was so happy I made the choice to move to South Beach, one of the best decisions of my life.

# "SAMADI" AKA SPIRITUAL AWAKENING

A *Samadi*, or a spiritual awakening is what I discovered I had experienced. It was a relief and shock yet I had to accept it as part of my journey.

The day of reckoning: Possession

The experience I am about to share was surely one for my journal, yet it posed a big problem, my writing was being disturbed, disrupted by "others" who want to write through me. I found out later the name for this phenomenon is called *Automatic Writing*. Pure obtrusion into my peaceful world of writing. My passion for life comes in the form of writing. Surely this was a joke or a sinister plot of my subconscious mind to stop me in my tracks.

On this night, November 6, 1996, six months to the day of meeting Yohvanni, my twin soul, a powerful windstorm blasted South Florida with gusts up to ninety miles an hour. It was appropriate for an eerie event to take place under these conditions, it would only create the background for a ghoulish scene. It was appropriate, because Halloween had been celebrated less than a week earlier.

I felt the change in the air and knew it was an extraordinary time yet, I had no idea what I was about to experience. The winds brought change indeed, at the most-deepest level of my existence or what I knew to be my existence. I revere this time with love for it raised my consciousness to a soaring level and since has been the most important event in my life.

I recall everything that transpired that night, yet it seemed like a total dream, a walking dream. Surreal was a word I had not ever used to describe my life until this ruptured my reality. I fully and respectfully understood the great works of art by the surrealist artists. Awakening to this new existence was not something I ever desired consciously, yet I co-created it so perfectly and distinctly. The experience I am about to describe is my awakening into the unconscious or unseen worlds.

I was blasted out of the physical world for a succession of days. I had the sense to document it as it happened. I will describe it and retell it from my perspective and my friends, who were there the whole time holding my hand. There is no amount of preparedness to achieve in my short lifetime for something like this. It was just not fathomable.

I can assure you we were all in shock for a long time after this experience. It all started with an exciting visit from my best friend from College, Rachelle. I had just moved to South Beach Miami after graduation and my bestie Rachelle, a school teacher like me, was on Thanksgiving Break. We planned a week-long vacation of beach activities. I lived on the prestigious Millionaires Row on the aqua blue Atlantic Ocean. Rachelle was so excited to come down and relax after a stressful teaching semester. After picking her up from the airport, I chose the casual *News Café* on Ocean Drive to sit down and catch up.

We had ordered a delicious cappuccino and talked for a few hours about the past year of our lives. We even reminisced about the very first day that we met. The level of intensity and shear shock that Rachelle felt was easily recalled. It was our first day in Dr. Silver's class. I walked in a little ruffled from the drive to school. I had just dodged a would-be stalker on the highway. I got up to speeds of almost ninety miles per hour to get away from him.

Last semester I took a class called Religions of the World. I desired to learn about the diverse religions and how they worshiped God.

One day I missed class and the next day, when I returned a student named John approached me. He said, "Hello, I noticed you were absent yesterday, I made a copy of the notes for you." I was shocked and pleasantly surprised. This was such a sweet gesture. He seemed to be a trustful person. Our friendship grew from this day. We swapped notes and had lunch on campus. I grew to appreciate his friendship very much. I did not think of him as anything more than a friend. He soon began to leave gifts on my car windshield and would show up when I least expected him to with lunch. I took all of this as a great friend showing appreciation. I would also buy lunch and be a good listener.

It quickly escalated and I began to feel smothered. I had to put distance between us. He even showed up uninvited at my home. I spoke to my mom and she called his parents and they explained he was not harmful and would tell him to keep away. Luckily, he graduated and I did not have to contend with him on campus any longer. My new Fall semester began and I got up early and eager to get to class on time.

I began driving to the *Garden State Parkway*, as I entered the onramp, I looked in my rearview mirror for other cars to safely merge. I noticed a car that was close behind mine. I proceed all the way to the left and accelerated. I then recognized that the car behind me belonged to John. My heart sank as I knew he was following me to see my schedule. I had received an email from him and I ignored it. This was so intrusive, I sped up to try to lose him and I almost crashed getting off another exit.

I did finally lose him. I made it to school, parked in the student lot, and ran to the teacher's building. I rushed into class and I grabbed the first open desk away from the door. All the new faces gave me the chills. I was so upset and now had to deal with orientation. I recalled my mind was racing as what to do about John? He was stalking me and I did not like it.

The next thing I know, a student behind me tapped my shoulder. I turn to my left and look at him, his hand went up and pointed to the door. I then turn to my right and looked at the classroom door. John was standing there calling me outside! The blood rushed to my head; I lost control. I jumped up and with my two hands flipped my desk upside down. All of the students freaked out! I didn't care. I walk towards the door and looked John right in the eyes. I said, "What the fuck are you doing?" He tried to answer, and I screamed. "Shut up! Shut up and turn around *now*!"

He did what I said, as he was timid, and I walked him out of the building. I threatened him with my pointy cowboy boots, and if he didn't continue to walk, I told him I would kick him. John tried several times to look back and I screamed. "Keep walking! I will kick you, *Keep walking*." It took forever to get him to the exit, but I succeeded on getting him out of the building. I pulled the door shut and went back to class.

I picked up the desk and carried on as if nothing happened. The teacher arrived shortly and by the end of class, we were separated into groups. I laughed to myself thinking how everyone was going to avoid me after that episode. Well, Rachelle and Tina and I were assigned to a group. Their faces were pale when they got the news. It worked out and we became the best of friends. We shared one tragic event. We went down the Jersey shore to *Bar Anticipation* to celebrate us graduating.

It was an amazing vibe, packed with people. Rachelle's boyfriend was with us as well. It was such an accomplishment. We had worked hard and long to earn our Bachelor's degree. We all were dancing on the dance floor when suddenly, I got pushed in my lower back so hard. I fell forward and almost hit my face on the floor. I somehow managed to maintain my balance, turned around to see this short girl staring at me with a mean face. I bent down to ask her. "Why did you push me?"

She gave me a dirty look and stuck her finger up at me. I then shoved her back. The next thing I knew, Tina who was behind me, pushed me to the floor. I was actually on the ground. I crawled a bit, then got up, and I saw people scattering. Rachelle found me. She screamed "Hurry up, go outside. Tina is hurt." I quickly ran outside and I saw Tina standing there with a sheet of blood covering her face, her big blue eyes were frozen in shock. She looked like *Carrie* in the scene when she was on the stage with pigs' blood poured on her. It was a vision I will never ever forget. I screamed. "What happened?"

She screamed at me. "Go get them. They are getting away!" I had four-inch platforms, which were very awkward. I jumped off the stairs and began running to the gravel filled parking lot. There were 3 girls running and the last one was slow. I barely caught up to her, I stretched out my arm to grab her, and at one point I felt her hair. I closed in and wrapped my right hand into her hair and dragged her to the ground. I had to hold her down and stopped the others from leaving the establishment.

A policeman came running towards me, and instead of reprimanding her, he arrested me. The situation got cleared up at the police station, as Tina and her father pressed charges on the girl who hit her in the head with a beer bottle. We found out they were from Brooklyn. Two sisters and a friend. It was a disaster to say the least. It was definitely an unexpected and unnecessary event to mark our Graduation from College. All three of us graduated and passed the Praxis Exam and went on to have successful teaching careers. With all this history, we need a great vacation experience to really celebrate! Miami is the perfect place to celebrate.

Rachelle and I drove back to my condo and prepared for sleep. I had to teach in the morning as I was a director of a learning center. My sleep patterns were very concise, I lay down and fall asleep with no hassle or issues. I am a great sleeper. I could drink an espresso at nine PM and be asleep an hour later. I was very exhausted as the day was filled with a lot of errands. I accomplished all of them and was eager to rest my body.

I recalled as I was laying on my right side, looking out my window feeling happy and fulfilled about being in such a lovely place in my life after leaving my life and home in New Jersey. I felt accomplished to have my best friend visit and show her the new life I created. I wanted to give her the greatest vacation ever.

Fifteen minutes had gone by and I was not sleeping. In fact, I tossed a bit since my right hand was tingling and almost numb. I moved it and felt it so tight and heated, my next thought was to get up and run it under cold water. I got up quietly as to not wake Rachelle, and ran cold water for a few minutes. Then dried it with a hand towel. I went back to bed laying on my back this time and was ready to win the sleep game.

Minutes went by and I felt my hand begin to vibrate and moving slightly. Each finger was jumping and fluttering in conjunction with the numbness I was feeling. It was now disturbing me, I thought seriously, maybe I was having a heart attack, but it was my right arm. I started to do a meditation prayer to focus on something else, and it worked. I finally fell asleep.

I awoke at 8:00 am and started my day, which began as normal as any other morning. I went into my office and reviewed my schedule, as per usual. I then got straight to work, grading diagnostic tests from the previous day. I was sitting quietly and peaceful for about ten minutes, then all of a sudden, my left hand got the same sensation I was feeling in my right hand the night before.

The feeling was disconcerting, as it reminded me again of last night, but this time being fully awake. I am left-handed writer, pen in hand but I couldn't quite feel it. At this point, I was confused and puzzled as to what to do. This was not so serious as to go to a hospital, yet it was concerning to say the least. I began to scan my body, seeing if I had any other sensations. I assessed it was an isolated sensation.

I needed to complete my work so I made a conscious decision to ignore the numbing sensation and continued grading my tests. The most incredible thing happened as I put my pen to the paper. My hand clumsily moved and marked the papers in an incoherent fashion. I was in shock sitting there staring at the paper. I got the idea to get a blank piece of paper and put my thoughts to paper. I sat back down and began to relax. I put the pen back in my hand, holding it as if I were going to write. Instantly, my hand started moving, drawing shapes, figures, and unruly lines, stars and scribbles. I continued to do this until the paper was filled.

I then released the pen, pushed myself away from the table, and put my hands on my knees in awe. I was processing what I had just experienced and it frightened me so much, I ran out of my office and went to sit in my car. I was distraught and did not know who to turn to or what to make of this. I reached for my phone and called my dear friend Tommy. He was a great friend and we respected each other.

I was shaking with fear and embarrassed to share what was happening, yet I knew he would be the one who can be rational and perhaps give me good advice. He met me for lunch nearby and as I soon as I greeted him, I began to cry. I hysterically shoved the paper in his face, telling him to look at what I drew. He was confused. All he could do is console me.

Once he heard the full story, he asked me to take a deep breath. I did and was able to discuss what had happened. He said the he wasn't sure what this was all about but as long as I was okay things would work out. I did feel better and things were back to normal for the time being. We laughed a lot and enjoyed our time.

I went back to the office and did not dare tell anyone else what had happened. In fact, I did not desire to finish the scoring of my tests. I went to the teaching floor to work with students. I was so distracted in a positive way that I forgot all about it. The children made me smile, laugh, and so happy to be there. Education is my passion and love to be immersed in it. My ten-hour day ended close to nine PM. I headed back toward South Beach to meet my Giordana and my Rachelle.

We began cooking a hearty meal and as we sat waiting at the dining table, I told them both I had something to tell them. This is phase two of the drama that was beginning to unfold like a flower with teeth as petals. They were excited and eagerly awaited my story. I went into my room and checked my hands to see what I was feeling. The numbing sensation was still there but tolerable. We ate our delicious dinner and chatted all about our day.

It was my turn to talk about what had happened. I explained in my casual way of joking way and they laughed when expected and then their eyes opened wide with excitement. I pulled out the drawing and showed them. They had a curious look I had never seen before. There was a dark energy of magic happening and now we all were aware. I also recalled a story my roommate Giordana told me she experienced an unexplained evil spell. She spoke of a time when she was just seven years old, playing in her living room in Manheim, Germany when all of sudden time stood still and she was frozen in her tracks.

She could see her mom in the distance and out from the ether three old woman appeared in front of her. They spoke to her in a weird language reciting something, and then they disappeared. She would absolutely attest from that moment on, she never felt the same after their visit. Giordana was convinced they put a spell on her because after this meeting her life was filled with one tremendous tragedy after another. She experienced several near-death incidents. She was abandoned by her father; her childhood friend had been raped and murdered. Giordana was no stranger to outer experiences so I knew the twinkle in her eye was sincere. She was crying, sitting on her hands and knees by the end at this new ordeal. I will get to that soon enough.

Giordana, Rachelle, and I sat on the couch after dinner trying to decipher what was happening to me. Giordana decided to play a game called "guess what I am thinking". She said if a spirit is here, they would know things. We laughed at the same time and agreed to play the game. Giordana, being the witty German, decided to ask a question I did not know the answer to. I only met her eight months earlier so I did not know much about her past or people in her past. Her suggestion was she would silently ask a question and I would write the answer.

Rachelle was quite amused but not sure what she was feeling about this game. Giordana asked the question and seconds later my hand began to write out a name, a German name. I thought Giordana's eyes were going to bulge out of her head. We both looked at her reaction and our eyes bulged out and now all three of us were tingling with a combination of fright, fear, and excitement.

Giordana quickly ran into her room and shut the door. Shella and I were still sitting on the couch staring at each other in silence. I stood up and walked into the kitchen to get a drink and process what happened and I noticed both hands were tingling now. True fear set in at this moment, for it was an uncharted territory for me to even fathom. To reorganize my thoughts and realize the "other side" might be communicating through me took a serious moment to swallow. This was only the beginning, and it ended with the sun rising up inside a Catholic Church on South Beach.

My arms were being electrically charged with what could be described as a pully system, lifting them up. I was trying so hard to keep them down, this force was growing and growing and it was trying to control me. I lost control of myself. I let fear in and that is when this force took hold. I was begging for Giordana and Rachelle to push my arms down. They both began to push my arms and could not get them down.

I ran into my room, arms raised as I sat on my bed in pure panic. I began screaming with a thunderous voice that penetrated the walls and my legs began to lift up with such ease. I then screamed. "Get a bible, help me, help me!" I screamed with both arms and legs up in the air. I could not do one leg lift. This was a full-blown attack and invasion of my body and soul. There was no bible anywhere. I kept thinking I needed a bible in between my tortuous screams. I felt completely exhausted and distressed. Two hours later and my arms were still up. Giordana then called our other friend and we decided to get me out of the apartment.

They led me into the downstairs lobby bathroom. Once in there, I began talking in different voices, expressing thoughts in different personas and referring to myself in the third person. I found myself at the sink scrubbing my arms and hands raw, saying out loud. "Don't you want to help your friend Violet? We need to cleanse her." My friends stopped me from washing and then realized someone else was there. They began to ask this entity questions and she told them her name was Mary, and they needed to help us. Please help us over and over. In moments of clarity, I would say. "It is me – Violet, what is going on here? help me!" I finally screamed at my friends to take me to a church now!

It was now past midnight, well over three hours of this insane attack. I insisted they take my car and drive me to get a bible and to find a Catholic church. My poor friend visiting me was scared out of her mind, but she did what I asked. The spiritual bookstore was still open. She ran in, bought the bible, came back, and drove me to an old Catholic Church on Alton Road. We arrived and by this time my other friend met us there. Rachelle, Giordana, Ana, and our friend Felix are carrying me out of my car, as I was in hysterics. When we got to the door, as luck would have it, it was locked.

They began pounding on the door all shouting out. "Help, help!" Finally, after fifteen minutes of pounding, a priest, who was short with glasses came to the door. He peeked his head out and asked in Spanish, what is going on? I was on the ground now. I had urinated on myself earlier and I was screaming. Help me! Help me please!" The priest screamed. *"No drugas aqui!"*

At once, all four of my friends shouted back at him. *"No drugas aqui"*! There was deafening silence. So quiet the air was sliced with a laser into another dimension. The priest was hit with a resonance of truth that broke him out of his initial assessment. He quickly swung open the doors and let my friends carry me inside. He knew what was happening to me. They laid me on the cold marble floor and as I stared up at the beautiful ceiling, asking. "God, why me, why me?" My friends all circled around me, Giordana, Rachelle, Ana and Felix.

The priest told us to wait there and he ran to another part of the church. We were all just praying. He came back a few minutes later, knelt down next to me, and began to say prayer. He blessed my forehead, and handed me his cross to hold. I grasped it so tight and never let it go. In fact, I still have it today. I realized it was his cross from his ordainment. It is my reminder of this transformative ordeal, forever.

Finally, an older Latin lady came rushing in from a side door, we all look to her as if she is the savior. We all were so relieved to see her and she quickly directed where to move me. They walked me over, closer to the alter and sat me in a chair. She began her work with prayer and holy water, and from that point on, I was blown away. I was a participant in a movie. I watched from the back seat, and from inside me, I heard howling, growling sounds I never heard humanly possible. It was if I was my own Foley artist in a movie, responsible for its sound effects. The added sounds reverberating off the church walls echoed, each sound seemingly more eerie.

I stood up a few times while my torso thrust forward and back. All the time I screamed at the top of my lungs and from the bottom of my stomach. The woman then did what all movies suggest, and she dowsed me in holy water. The sensations felt like cold wax being poured on me. It made the spirits agitated, as I began to growl and she dowsed me again. She continued this for almost an hour, until I fell over in my chair. I was completely drained. My depleted body slumped in the chair and had no more screams left inside me. I was completely discharged of any life force. The woman directed my friends, in Spanish, to take me home to rest.

Trembling and shaking all of us in shock, we gathered ourselves and we drove home. It was over for now. I got home and I showered, changed and went to bed. The next day, I had many decisions to make. I was so confused as to what to do and where to go. It made no sense, yet made perfect sense, but not for someone like me. A Jersey Girl who moved away to make her own way, to be independent from family and create a new life in a place filled with nature, warmth and love.

Rachelle called my mother and informed her something had happened. My mother pleaded for get me home immediately. I made the decision to go home with my friend on a plane to New Jersey. I would return home to my mom. It was not very comforting but it was all I had.

The plane ride was creepy, since I had time to reflect all the way up the in the atmosphere. I kept asking why did this happen? I immediately felt consoled by someone other than me and they assured me I was going to be all right. Rachelle and I laughed and giggled and even took pictures of me with my bible. Thank goodness I had such a great sense of humor, or this would have ended me. I had such a huge ego, and this happening was like chopping down the biggest redwood tree in my ego forest. It was an unthinkable traumatic occurrence for my ego.

I was always so in control, teaching and counseling others, knowing what to do in every moment. It was almost as if I was an egomaniac who thought she was heading for glory and now she was going to the crazy house.

Through the shame and powerlessness, I found something I never would have found, a oneness with who I am. Arriving at my mom's made me sad. When I looked into my mom's eyes, she was unsure. She never looked at me like this before. In fact, I was the one who handled everything. I was the courageous and daring one, accomplishing anything I set my mind to doing. I didn't like the look on her face and I tried to explain what I think happened, without sounding insane. It shouldn't have gotten any worse, but it did.

I went to lay down in her room to sleep. I kept getting up and throwing up. It felt as though my body was purging but nothing was coming up but blood. I was in the bathroom for over an hour. My mom called was forced to call 911.

Adding further embarrassment to this drama, she ordered them to do bloodwork, because she thought I had taken drugs. To her surprise, the test came back negative for any type of illegal drugs. I was kept in the hospital for four days under surveillance. They had no real diagnosis except for the usual nervous breakdown and schizophrenia. I was disgusted by the thought of that prognosis, yet I knew many before me were cast into this category.

The mystery cause is never known, yet pills are prescribed to cover it up

Well, nothing was explained because there was no real cause for this to happen. All I knew is that I wanted to get back to Miami to begin my research and find the help I needed to put this experience in its proper perspective. Modern medicine could not explain this, no way, no how. I knew in my heart what I experienced was something that went beyond the realm of modern doctor's knowledge. I also knew there had to be someone would help me understand what had happened. I returned to beautiful Miami, now tainted with this horrible experience looming over me. I managed to stay strong and focused on getting back to work and living my life.

# QUESTIONS OF FAITH
# AND REALITY

All I had were questions. Why? What? How? I wanted to write so badly. I needed answers to soothe my soul. I wanted to explore my mind through written words. My journal writing had been my savior, my friend, my compassion in life for as long as I could remember. I would write all of my feelings, thoughts, and ambitions. I would also write queries to the Universe that perplexed me. This was the solution for my dilemmas. My writing was the catalyst for that outrageous occurrence and I feared to pick that pen up. I was deeply upset. A few days went by and I dared not touch the pen that lay by my beautiful journal.

On the third day, I felt amazing. All was back to normal at work and at home. I went back to running on the beach. I worked out at the gym and swam in the ocean daily. I was so happy to be with my co-workers and students. Lots of laughter and love pouring in effortlessly. It felt great. On the fourth night, I got home early so I cooked dinner for my roommate and me. We had an interesting conversation and laughed a lot.

After dinner, I settled in my room and had so many thoughts running through my head. I needed to write and to map out my path. I knew if I picked up my pen and began to write, if some unwanted energy showed up, it would destroy my peace. It would be a double-edged sword slicing through me, my mind. My anxiety turned slightly into anger. I wanted to be free to be me, to do what I wanted without fear.

I sat staring at my journal for thirty minutes or so. I went to the kitchen and ate a piece of German chocolate to see if it would replace my desire to write. I then walked out on the balcony to see the beautiful bay water shimmering with peace and tranquility. I felt defiant, almost fearless, and decided to turn to a new page in my journal to conquer my fears. I wrote and wrote words flowing, healing and cleansing my mind of these deep thoughts. It was glorious and amazingly fun and invigorating. I will never be separated from my expressions again.

I let flow, all of my soul's queries and it was like liquid metal, my hand gliding across the pages. With all my heart and soul, I wrote. I wrote to release the pain and to revere all that I am, was, and ever shall be. I wrote to feel alive and to make sense of the illusions. I reached nearly the bottom of the second page and suddenly, my hand was gripped with tension and that all too familiar feeling of fuzzy vibrations.

My hand was overtaken, something was trying to write through me. I gasped and threw the pen and journal. I jumped up and went to my window to look toward the water to calm me. Fear set in and I realized I was not free or healed from this spiritual drama. I finally decided to tell my roommate this entity was back.

I knocked on her door, now locked due to her fear of me. I spoke through the door and said, "Do not be alarmed but the energy is here. I just tried write in my journal." I told her I would go to the hospital tomorrow to see what I can learn about this phenomenon. I expressed I could not live like this, walked away toward my room with deep sadness.

I heard her door open and I turned to her crying as she came toward me and said, "While you were away, Ana found someone to help you." Ana was from Brazil. From the night of possession, she declared this happened a lot in Brazil. Her mom was aware as she told her everything that happened. I was shocked to hear this news.

When Ana told me over the phone the person was located here

in Miami, I screamed with joy. I got the number from her and stared at it. Could this person save me? His name was Dr. Tom Norris, a Psychologist and Spiritual Healer. I called as if he was the only person on the planet that could help me get my life back. I needed insight as to what was happening to me. He answered on the third ring.

I was so relieved to hear a calm, stable, loving voice on the other end. I explained who I was and he assured me he would be able to help me. He told me I had some lost souls attached to me and we will remove them. He sounded so sure about this and I was just a frightened child grasping at anyone who claimed to help. My faith was all I had and the trust in my friends for seeking help for me. It was worth a try as the alternative was being admitted.

I made the appointment for eleven AM the next morning. When I hung up the phone, I was so relieved with a sense of normalcy pending. Driving on the highway to Dr. Norris's office was a thrill. I felt like I was going to pick up a million dollars in cash. Freedom has no price, but I would take whatever he was giving. I recalled feeling the most joy I had felt in two weeks. I recognized I was in an unauthorized area of existence and I was simply a novice. I just needed a master to show me teach me the way of this spirit world. Dr. Tom Norris was that master. I chose him and he chose me, for this was the path necessary for my enlightenment.

# TOUCHING THE LIGHT OF GOD

I arrived at his office and he was standing outside, he guided me into the driveway. I was so happy to see a tall bright eyed, warm friendly fellow greeting me. I had no idea what a spiritual healer would look like but he was as normal as they come. Better than normal, perfect. We greeted each other and he led me into his study.

I sat down and took note of my surroundings. There were beautiful posters of mystical characters and deities. A large wall of books, and rosewood incense filled the room. I felt safe and for once, throughout this ordeal, I felt understood. Tom sat across from me with a yellow notepad and pen, he began to ask me some background questions.

Dr. Norris detected with certainty there were lost souls interfering in my aura. He said they needed to be released to the light, as they were lost and had found an opening in my aura. My face was blank, until I gasped in disbelief. Dr. Norris explained this happens very often, not to worry.

I looked wildly at this man and he quietly said it will be painless. I thought for a quick second. "Is he sane? The opposite is I am insane, so why not go for it!" I basically had no other hope. If it worked out smoothly, I win. If not, I am back where I started. I was willing to explore and allow his knowledge to heal me.

I took a deep breath and leaped into faith, willing to follow his direction. He said to sit comfortably and relax. He began the session with prayers honoring all of the great masters of light. Jesus, Buddha, Brahman, Mary, Moses, Archangels of sorts, and invited them to the session. My eyes were closed, but I peeked open to see if I could see them. This would have blown my mind even further, but I could not see them.

I recalled feeling a deep peace and calm overtake the room. Dr. Norris was armed with love and began with this question. "Who is here with Violet?" There was silence for a moment and then a tightening in my throat area, I began to speak. Words were forming and I was just in awe that I could be there in my body but not in control of speaking. Same as the night of possession.

The spirit began to speak, he said. "Michael is my name".

The dialogue began. "Why are you bothering Violet?

The spirit answered him saying she reminds me of someone I used to know. Dr. Norris explained to him it goes against Cosmic Law to interfere with a human's life force. Michael began to get upset and told Dr. Norris he wasn't going anywhere because he had nowhere else to go. Tom assured him there was a beautiful place to go and by imposing on me, he would only prolong his arrival.

Dr. Norris told the spirit he belonged in the light where all of his loved ones were waiting for him. The spirit aggressively protested and I felt his anger and discontent. My throat tightened and my body jolted from side to side. "I don't belong there, I am bad, I am bad and I can't go to the light. I killed my girlfriend and I did very bad things to others."

I was getting alarmed, yet this over protective energy was covering me. I peeked my eye open to see if Dr. Norris was still there and nothing had changed. I was feeling confident and closed my eye again as I sat back. Dr. Norris, after a moment of silence, spoke clearly and confidently. "Michael, you can be forgiven for all you have done here on Earth. Look around you, do you see who is here for you?"

Michael then gasped wildly looking up and around using my head and eyes. He spoke slowly and softly this time. "I can see Jesus and Buddha and other beings in the distance and there is light."

Dr. Norris said. "That is correct. We are all here to assist you to reunite you with your loved ones in the light. The only thing you need to do is forgive yourself for all you have done and you will be redeemed. It is your choice to stay or to unite with the universal light. Either way you will not be able to stay with Violet. You can choose right now and we will all guide you safely to the light."

This spirit had gusto. or shall we say a very forceful nature. I was very anxious to remove this one. Dr. Norris began to explain the process of life and death or the return to the light. I was listening to every word and it was intriguing. He said all souls have a chance to redeem themselves at death and after, and this opportunity was his for the taking.

My arms were up in the air, exhausted from this presence taking up space within me. He was still resistant to what Tom was saying. Next, Tom asked Michael to look up and tell him what he saw. My head tilted up. He was reacting to the sensation of sight. My throat tightened and I was reminded to give up control. Michael excitedly said. "I see my mom!"

Tom assured him it was her and she was waiting for him to return. There was an immediate shift in energy. My body felt lighter and I knew we were close to getting Michael to the light. I did not understand all of this, but what a beautiful experience/ritual to guide lost souls to the light. Once seeing his loved ones, he began to trust Dr. Norris more. Michael was able to see that he was in a place called purgatory.

Souls who have died suddenly or have done bad things are frightened or turned away from going to the light. It is simply due to them judging themselves. The thought anyone who has done heinous acts or just evil people can be forgiven. The Catholic church called this penance.

To ask God for forgiveness, to confess and seek restoration. This was the basis of this ritual. The guidance specifically said if you are truly sorry and can forgive yourself, you can be saved and returned to the light. I fully understood the process and honored this experience so much. To be the source of releasing a living being, out of a place called limbo into a purification ritual reuniting them with where we all come from.

I would never be the same or see life the same way after that day. I finally understood for those two weeks of suffering, confusion, shame, grief, embarrassment, pain, and stress, I was given this remarkable gift. I engaged in a great cause that was bigger than anything I had ever been a part of in my life time.

I felt very warm and compassionate toward these pained souls, for their suffering and now to their enlightenment. I could hardly stand the excitement and wondered why I had stayed so calm and relaxed, which allowed me to follow through with our mission to return this soul home to the light.

The process Dr. Norris explained, was visualization. He asked everyone who were present – the souls and ascended masters – to visualize white light coming up from the ground, through my feet and up my legs, he asked all of us to do this in unison. I began to do this exactly and I recalled feeling a heated sensation on my legs and this heat moved all the way up my torso. He noted each chakra as the light passed through, as it slowly, gracefully, lifted this soul upward and out, to eventually unite with the energy that created him.

As we got to my heart chakra, I felt a strong tug, and pressure for a while, then it shifted a bit and then I felt a heavy energy sitting in my chest and lower neck. I was straining, holding this ball of pure wild energy, my arms stretched as far up as they could reach. Vibrations in my palms, as they faced up releasing and collecting energy. In this moment I wished I was able to see what was happening,

I was sweating, working arduously to ascend this soul, breathing heavily, for this force was strong and I had been containing it at the gateway between two worlds. I kept steady and strong. Love and awe were the only emotions I felt. It had been almost forty-five minutes and he was stuck. Exhausted, I wanted to be done with this insanity. I wanted to make it all go away. Michael, Dr. Norris, and this two-week ordeal. Deep breathing and drinking water helped me regain my focus and dedication to the mission.

Dr. Norris realized he was stuck and asked him another question. "Michael, can you look at your heart and tell me what you see?"

Through my eyes, Michael looked down and he said in an angry voice. "I see nothing. It is all black. I am all black, I see nothing."

Tom said. "Look again closer." My head tilted down and he was actually looking and said he saw a white dot. Dr. Norris quickly exclaimed. "*Yes*, that's it! You have it. You, like all of us were born with it and will always have it. The white light from which you came into this world. Your heart holds the light! You have lived a harsh life full of dark deeds and habits. Throughout your time here you have accumulated darkness and it has covered all of your light. We are going to transform that now."

Tom asked everyone to visualize the white speck in his heart chakra growing bigger and bigger. We all began to visualize the white speck of light growing and suddenly I felt soothing heat in my heart flowing and tears came to my eyes. I knew Michael must have felt this, too. We were all witnessing a total transformation from dark to light.

Michael looked down and said it was getting larger, and I felt myself getting lighter. This was just astounding to experience. I was in the similar position, with my arms stretched up to the sky, head tilted back and feeling the beautiful light. I began sensing we were very close. I asked for strength to endure the pain in my arms.

As if something more amazing could take place, what happened next was the single most fantastic experience I have ever known to this day. Unachievable by all physical science and the laws of physics. I was not prepared for it, yet it was meant for me and it changed my life forever. Breathing heavier and feeling the pressure of a boiling pot of water, we were almost there, this beautiful group effort. It was like the last yard of a race, where everyone is rooting for the winner.

We were all at the brink of collapse, all energy on this one goal, sweat, tension, heart beating and kaboom! I exploded back into the chair, my arms flailing about I began laughing beyond all control. I was gasping, laughing, giggling, breathing loudly, beaming, shaking, and vibrating. I was in this state of bliss for over 2 minutes and finally, when I caught my breath, my eyes were wide open. I started to focus and there was Tom sitting calmly in his chair with the biggest grin. I could not speak, so with my eyes asked. "What just happened"?

"Do you know what just happened to you?"

I was holding my chest as it felt like my heart energy field was twenty feet in front of me. I replied. "No what just happened"?

Tom, without hesitation, said. "My dear, you have touched the light!"

I was shocked at this news but even more shocked at the feeling. It over took my whole being and I felt as though my whole body was plugged into electricity. It felt as if every cell, atom, molecule was experiencing an orgasmic blast that riveted my soul beyond comprehension. I had been immersed in pure white light energy. This feeling was so divine. I could never describe in words how I felt. I attempted to describe it by saying it felt as though I was being electrocuted by love. I wanted to know more about what I just encountered.

I knew there was no going back to who I was before. I was connected with my purpose and I wanted to live it fully. I thanked Dr. Norris for assisting me and most of all, I joked with my savior he had miraculously healed my tortured soul from some sort of mild form of Schizophrenia.

He laughed and explained many patients who have spirit interference had a break in their aura. The souls could then get in and manipulate the living soul. A break in the auric field can be caused by extreme emotions and traumas. I was so relieved and filled with joy and a deep sense of happiness. My first question to Dr. Norris was. "How did they get in?" He asked me if I suffered any recent trauma. I said, "Not at all. I have an amazing life and just met the man of my dreams. I am in love, have an amazing job, live on the ocean and have great friends."

I left his office perplexed, yet as I was driving home, I recalled the day I met Yohvanni, my twin flame. It was as though my soul escaped out of my aura field to me with his soul, left frozen until it returned back to me. I was convinced this was the cause of my possession. It was eight months prior to the possession. This was the only recent semi-traumatic event I experienced. But was that considered trauma?

Dr. Norris confirmed the connection between Yohvanni and I could have been the reason for the break in my aura. To me, it did not matter after that experience. Dr. Norris trained me how to protect myself from unwanted souls. I used discernment and a few techniques to close my channels. I became so compassionate and loving toward the world. I truly transformed for the better. I was now privy to knowing my soul's purpose. I was in deep peace and tranquility.

Returning back to South Beach was pretty amazing for I was singing and laughing again and all was back to normal. Well at least normal as in not crazy but 'special". I was so ecstatic over this experience I cried and laughed all the way home. I rushed up to our apartment and burst through the door to tell Giordana what just happened. We went to eat at the café by the ocean and reveled in the thought the spiritual world was real, and not made up in movies, dreams and fantasies.

We were privy to the whole experience from start to finish. We both felt relief as to the closure of our mystical and traumatic ordeal. This was just the beginning for me. My journey as a healer and intuitive began. I was shown how to heal, to be more factual, I possessed a knowing of how to heal using deep compassion and intuition. It was a beautiful gift bestowed upon my soul.

I felt truly honored, but also hesitant. After a while I did embrace it as I had no choice in the matter. I was healing and speaking with love and my eyes expressed love for all humanity. I had always from a child expressed great love for people, children, and animals. This was a divine expression of love I had never reached or experienced.

I was floating as I walked and felt so electric with God's love. People showed up and I was able to heal them. I didn't tell anyone I was a healer it just organically happened. I found this so strange. I was a magnet to those in need of healing. Magic, bliss, pureness, protection, and love was all I could feel for four years. I was assigned healing of souls with bodies and souls without.

I ascended many souls to the light. Souls that were in limbo hanging around the firmament. I was asked to heal their traumas and teach them the light is the way to transcend. I explained the souls that die suddenly by accident or murder are often left in between dimensions. After my beautiful experience I knew first-hand how powerful the light was. It is a pure beam of love light particles taking all the pain and all the bad memories and replacing it with bliss.

It was an honor to assist souls to the next level. It was a difficult job at first, and took a bit to understand the importance. When I began channeling young children that had passed in a car crash, they would describe the incident and began crying, as I would begin feeling their fear and pain. It was heartbreaking and soul breaking indeed.

I recalled a cute conversation I had with a young boy. I saw the vision he described as he spoke through me, telling me of the accident with his mom. He described seeing himself rise up over the car. He asked me if there was music in heaven. I said yes! I told him the light of heaven has music and all you need to feel blissful. We chatted for a while and when he was ready, I told him I would show him the way.

This was my usual task upon hearing when a lost soul communicated with me. I learned how to tune in and tune out. It was quite a daunting task yet I became so good at counseling souls. I have journals of writings from many cases. Towards the end of my assignment, I was sending up souls in groups.

It was easier and necessary for time constraints here in the Earth Plane. Just to give you an idea of what I was doing in conjunction with healing souls, I was working full time as a teacher and bartending at a local restaurant, clocking in a full seventy hours in a week. I would do my healing at night after dinner and school work. I was truly exhausted. I finally decided after three years, I needed a break and desired to change my whole life around. I decided to quit teaching, as there was no significant pay and the bartending job was a dead end.

I was nearing thirty years old and wanted a new career. I began to study for my Real Estate License. I completed the course and passed the test within a week. I was so excited to start on this journey. It was the best decision I ever made. I jumped right in and began selling time shares.

I realized I was not this type of a salesperson. I was a compassionate caregiver with a huge consciousness of cause and effect. I was not ready for the tactics and lack of consciousness it took to be the top sales person. I struggled so much and cried because I could not lie and convince people to purchase. I did learn so much about sales and life. I did not give up on my dream to be a Real Estate Agent.

I continued on and began a position as an assistant to a top producer. I knew I had much to learn about the critical steps in selling/

purchasing homes. I positioned myself in a boutique Company with a true professional. He taught me all the tricks of the trade and I proved to be a great realtor. I dreamed of one day owning my own home on South Beach. I made sure I learned as much as I could each day.

# TIME FOR GROWTH

I began a journey of self-discovery via a world-renowned course called *The Landmark Forum*. I was so excited to complete my *Landmark Forum Course*. It was grueling, yet the most mind-altering experience I have had to this date. A phenomenal look inside your core being, your personality traits, habits, and most of all, your excuses to being fully expressed. This course was right up my alley. How it came to me was very auspicious.

Giordana, whom I had not spoken to in many years, walked into my real estate office and asked to speak with me. I was so shocked and frozen to see her, as we had a falling out. I quickly brought her into my office and listened to what she had to say. She began to tell me of this amazing experience she had in a course. Giordana's eyes were almost bulging out of her head and her voice was so high pitched. It looked like she was on a high from what she discovered.

She then apologized – sort of – and coyly invited me to her graduation. I was so intrigued, I quickly said yes. It was to be on a Tuesday evening, as all graduations are held. It was a large gathering of people and I was intimidated at first. Everyone smiled and greeted me, as I put on my name tag. We were seated together. As I looked across the sea of faces, I was suddenly filled with fear. The keynote speaker took command and after putting the guests at ease, he began calling on the graduates, asking them what did they get out of *The Landmark Forum*?

Many hands were raised in unison. The results some of the participants shared were so outstanding memories that were on the edge of unbelievable. I sat in amazement listening to these testimonies. I felt so many things at once. I witnessed joy, possibility, oneness, forgiveness, abundance, and peace. Everyone who spoke had a sense of peace on their face, or should I say relief?

I felt all the emotions as they were expressed and knew this was something I would like to experience. I signed up for the course but did not take it until months later. I had to save my money and my schedule was filled up, but I had to make room to attend the three-day event. I completed the course and graduated in October of 2003.

It was life altering, mind exploding, and a definite success in my journey in this life. Once a person takes this course, they evolve so quickly. Participants become super human, or the super highest version themselves. You are asked to participate in exercises that reveal the most crucial parts of your existence. You are shown truths of your current reality that break the beliefs that were handed down or inherited, and in an instant, you are freed from that reality.

The relief comes when you realized how you created everything in your life. The good, bad, and ugly. You are the one you have been waiting for. *The Landmark Forum* is only the first part in a series of courses offered. I attended all the following courses to complete the program. The last course is where I manifested Vlad. I created a monster and he came to life. I thought I was creating someone beautiful and filled of compassion, creative, fun, loving and my forever love.

To explain, the last course is where you write down all of your possibilities and create from a powerful space of knowing and true desire. In this course, I wrote down all of my requirements to a tee. I left no details to chance. I was ready, willing, and determined to reach my ultimate goals in my life.

I was so excited because this was the first time, I put aside fear. I was able to dream dreams that were so much bigger than the world from which I came. This was my chance to prove to myself and anyone who was watching, that I could achieve my dreams. I wrote down in our Course Guide I would be purchasing a home by December 2006. I gave myself six months to create this dream come true. I would have $100,000 in my bank account. I would manifest my soulmate for life. He would be into Real Estate like me, love to dance, love the beach, have a great sense of humor, and be tall, handsome and fit.

# ROOMMATE WANTED

I was sharing a beautiful two-bedroom apartment on Collins Avenue. with an Italian roommate named Alex.

He worked as a restaurant manager on the Ocean drive. Alex was a super character unable to be defined by his Italian accent and suit. One day he bared his soul and shared his life's dream with me. I recalled laughing at first, which thankfully I stopped before I started. He said he wanted to be a cowboy. I said, "You came all the way from Italy to America to fulfill this dream?"

He said yes. This was his intention and final destination was the Midwest. We lived together for about a year, until he gave me his notice! He was on his way to Texas to live out his childhood dream. The best part of living at the *Alamac*, was being a block from the ocean and from the famous *Mansion Club*. Alex leaving was perfect timing to allow for this disaster to happen. Was it all divine timing?

I was now seeking to find the perfect person to occupy the second bedroom. I put ads out on the

Internet, and low and behold, I received a DM that said "Hey". Our communication began and it was more business than flirty yet his profile picture showed an incredible amount of abs. They were definitely worth looking at for a while. I wondered if they were real or if he was even real.

He was contacting me from Orlando, Fl. He asked if he could come see the apartment and we set up a meeting. Vlad was supposed to come view the apartment but had to cancel. Vlad was still interested in moving to South Beach and I was willing to give him a chance.

I had another prospect come by and she paid me, so I rented her the room. I had to break the news to Vlad. He understood and suggested he should still come by and meet each other. I was sure this was his plan from the start. To live rent free in my apartment. Of course, this is what magically happened. It was also the biggest downfall in my life with this one bad decision.

I wish I knew ahead of time how bad this was going to get. He drove up in a shiny royal blue Jaguar, light leather interior. He looked so handsome and studious with his deceiving glasses. I was instantly attracted to him. It was a night to remember. I wanted to know more and see more of him. He had a shy boy innocence, yet combined with a rough edge.

He proclaimed he was straight edge, which he had to explain. I was ten years his senior. I have never heard of the term. He explained that straight edge meant he never took drugs or drank. I admire refrain in a person and he definitely had that attribute. Our relationship started off slowly, but accelerated very quickly. After a week, we were discussing buying property together.

It was all so fast, yet I had intentionally set out to find my life partner. I really thought this was my manifestation. I truly believed God had sent me a divine partner. I was all in and was willing to give all I had, to receive the gift of true love. Looking into his dark sadistic psycho eyes, in retrospect, was life changing. The veil of his love had many hidden disguises. Love energy which gives life also takes it from someone.

Unsurprisingly, it happened so quickly with the love bombing and doting attention. Emails of devoted love to continue the farse of being the one. One minute we were driving on my scooter all over South Beach enjoying the weather and the newness of meeting, and the next we were talking about buying property together. I felt overwhelmed and unable to process it all.

The meeting with his father was what I call the seal the deal meeting. I recalled him looking into my eyes and saying. "I am Papa Vlad, I going to help you". That was the first lovely phrase burned in my mind from Papa.

From the beginning they sought me out as a business deal and used the two-part closer technique. How sick and demented it all was and the complete set up of an innocent human being. I actually prepared myself for purchasing and developing myself as more than just a real estate assistant. I was seeking to expand my knowledge and build my future wealth.

Low and behold, the internet was just the place to seek a potential roommate or a psychopath surfing the web seeking out a specific type of person. This was an easy thing to do on AOL. One can read the profile, type of work and find exactly the person you are seeking. I do know one of the criteria they required was to be a licensed Realtor with good credit. That was enough to get them out of debt and homelessness. I lent his parents $1000 within a month of meeting Vlad. I feel ashamed now to say I was a "lay down". I truly was blindsided by the prospect of securing my dreams. I would have given a kidney. Looking at this in hindsight, knowing how innocent my heart was, I felt a deep sadness. Since this great loss, I have not opened up my heart to anyone. I lost so much love in my life and I really needed this relationship to work.

I lost hope I would ever get my dream of true love and connection. I looked in my journal and I gave a name to my person. It was a vision paired with a name. I called it "ultra love". I wrote it all over my journals, from twenty-five until thirty-five, when I met Vlad. My vision was us holding hands, rising up to the top of the Earth, powerful light searing through us, raising our love energy that covered the Earth. I drew my visions and was sure God had delivered him. How could I not think it?

We wrote down our dreams together and he assured me he loved me in so many ways. We had fun and laughed and created things together. I just didn't fathom he was playing me until the moment, the finale of their unimaginable deed.

# THE LION'S DEN

Vlad and I have purchased a beautiful Mediterranean home on South Beach. I obtained the loan and put the deposit down. Vlad father created an assignment of equity to ensure we receive money back at closing. We moved into the house and immediately started to decorate and furnish our home. It was the most amazing experience. Vlad and I went all over to pick the best furnishings. He was able to put up all of the chandeliers and the two 10 foot mirrors on either side of our fireplace. The ceilings were 14ft tall with beautiful beams. I recall Vlad installing a 100-pound brass chandelier all by himself. It had beautiful cherubs holding the lights. I thought he was super human at times. We had a movie room with a 120-inch retractable screen. I bought a beautiful handmade hammock for the front porch. I was truly the happiest I had been in a very long time. I was not willing to give up this dream for anything.

It was five AM and Vlad came home. We were together earlier and I left and went home. I was upset and not feeling like being social. When he arrived, he was drunk and being aggressive. I was startled and I lashed out at him, pushing him off of me. He attacked me, and I tried to run out of my home, almost making to the street. I feel his large hand grab my hair and throw me to the ground.

Vlad had mounted me, with his knees bracing my arms down. He then slipped into a demonic rage, as he stared down at me. I saw his eyes switch over. Down came his forceful slap, then another, and another. He repeatedly used his hand as a pendulum. He slapped me from side to side, hand raising high up. I could hardly breathe, screaming. "Vlad, Vlad, Vlad stop, *please stop*!"

To no avail, he could no longer hear me or see me. Deep into a black-eyed rage. I was giving up, and all of a sudden, I hear a loud voice scream into my right ear, "*Scream for water now*!" I came to after hearing it and immediately, I screamed. "*Vlad, I need water! Water! Vlad*!" Instantaneously, he broke out of his rage looked down as in complete shock as to what he was doing.

He jumped up off of my body and ran into the house. I quickly ran for my life down the street in my underwear to a phone booth on Lincoln Road, and franticly called 911. The police showed up and he was nowhere to be seen. I had him arrested.

The next thing I know is I was being threatened by his father. They coerced me to write a letter to the judge saying I was lying. I was truly scared for my life. All three showed up at my home. I was alone they all forced me to pack a bag, saying we were going to Key West for the week. I did what they said. I was totally under their control. I was bruised all over my face. It took two weeks to heal. His plan was to take me down to Key West to recover so no one would see me. I recalled wearing a hat and sunglasses the entire time I was in Key West. I felt as though I had left my body. I was with him doing things, seeing things yet feeling nothing. As if all of this was enough, Vlad forced me to have sex with him. I gave in to his demands, but again, I felt nothing. I was not alive after his attack. My poor soul went into retreat. I walked around like a zombie. The violation to my soul and body was more than I could ever withstand.

I felt lost, broken into a million pieces and, most of all, shamed of what I had become. An abused woman, being locked down by a psychopath and his parents. I was sure water saved my life and to me God is Water. I would surely be dead or brain damaged if he continued. The voice in my right ear saved me. It gave me the strength to go on as

I knew I was being protected. I did not know why but the support my angel gave me was enough to be allegiant.

There is a phrase used to describe the eventual loyalty you feel toward your abuser, it is the Stockholm syndrome. I felt like a prisoner, yet I was compelled to love him. I fought hard not to, yet he would come and push his way into my energy, into my mind. He would use brainwashing techniques, holding my face and making me stare into his eyes while he abused me with his demeaning words and unloving touch. It was truly a living hell.

I now understood the full scope of what these evil people were doing. I was a straw buyer for them. I was targeted to purchase a property so they could pull out the equity of the home at the closing table. It was a legal transaction and I understood how it worked. Papa Vlad looked into my eyes and said, "Trust me". I trusted him, I truly believed he had our best interest at heart. I never saw the proverbial sledge hammer coming down on my head. They were all in on it. I was in the dark as to how many times they did this before to other victims, and many victims came after me. They all played their roles convincingly.

I recalled a time we all went to North Carolina and the parents bought a book for us, the Book of Vlad and Violet. It was a pre-written, cute novel using our names. They really knew how to make everything seem so real. I wish I could have ripped off their masks to see what lived inside their ugly hearts and souls. The scheme was so perfectly planned by them. I was in LaLa land thinking of my dreams coming true.

Vlad played the part of property scout. He found properties that had equity in them, and his Papa, with the same name, was equipped with a legal document called an Assignment of Equity. The equity could only go to a third party for repairs such as a contractor or manager. If you guessed it, you are smart. Papa Vlad was the one to receive the equity in the home I purchased. The home had almost $87,000 in equity. I applied for stated income loan. I was the sole owner of the home. Their fake plan guaranteed we would pull out the equity and use it to make payments and repairs. Papa Vlad said he would give us the money back after we closed. He kept all the equity.

I will never forget the day of reckoning. I called several times that day, as my mortgage was due and we did not have enough funds. Papa did not answer any of my calls. I was beginning to panic as my name was on the home, my credit was at stake, and if one is late just once, it calls attention to the banks. This day was the day I lost my mind. It was the rudest awakening for they revealed their whole plan.

I began to argue with Vlad. I asked him where his father was and why he was not putting the money in my account to pay our mortgage. He got defensive and started yelling, saying he don't know why. I called Papa Vlad several more times and left nasty messages. By this time, I knew what was happened. I really just wanted to hear it. My heart and head were spinning in such pain. I was betrayed, lied to, and left to run wild in my mind of what would happen to everything I had built.

I received the final blow the next day. I called numerous times, and he finally answered. He said, "I don't have the money, you better figure something else out!" He hung upon me, that was the last piercing phrase burned in my mind from Papa Vlad.

I fell to the floor because I knew my life was destroyed. I have been had by a three-ring crime family. Everything I thought was real, was shattered in that instant. All the love and the trust I had for Vlad dissolved instantly. I could not look at his face with trust again. He and his father and mother were just monsters posing as human beings. They had evil intentions all planned out years before they met me.

They had been doing this scam to many others. I now had to figure how to survive this disgraceful fall. My life as I knew it was over. I had a $7000 mortgage to pay with no help and all my equity gone to a psychopathic family. All I could remember was the beautiful night Vlad and I went roller blading and he said, "Let's go see the house I found for us." I was so excited, as we skated down Lincoln Road to get there. He had me close my eyes when we got closer. He then pulled me under the beautiful arched Ficus hedge that lined the front of the house. I opened my eyes and there was the most beautiful Spanish Mediterranean Home. We kissed under the arch, I felt so complete. I was really going to have my dreams come true.

We skated back to the *Alamac* on Thirteenth and Collins to have dinner. It was all a lie. It was all a game for them to put money into their wretched hands. They bought two homes with the money in Tamarac Florida. Meanwhile I would soon be homeless. I watched the movie, *Switching Places*, with Eddie Murphy and realized that was their goal. To steal what I had and make their life better. Not one single care was given as to what would happen to me. They were heinous. I pity their souls.

# CRASH OF 2008

The market crash devastated my Real Estate business. At the same time, my lifes dream is crashing. My investments dissolved and I was wiped out of savings with no potential earnings. My sister Damiana and her husband saw this as a perfect time to pressure me to sign my name off of my childhood home. I begged her to stop harassing me. I was in an abusive relationship and the market crashed left me in both panic and under duress. She even frightened my mother. Damiana said. "If Violet's properties go into foreclosure, they will come after our home."

My mother was sickly at this time and called me to tell me how Damiana was pressuring her. My mom even cried one day. She said, "Please Violet, sign the papers." I explained no one can take your home. I received pressuring emails and phone calls from both of them. I finally gave in on the premise I would calm their fears of anyone taking our childhood home. I did this freely thinking it didn't matter if my name was on the deed. I trusted this agreement was to protect our childhood home. I always assumed I would still be considered a 1/3 owner, I trusted this was only to protect the home where we grew up.

I continued to rely on Vlad and his parents for a while as the market crashed right when I signed the papers to my childhood home. They went on to enhance their lives as mine deteriorated. Vlad continued to degrade me and attack me physically. I was living in a home he could break into at any time he desired. I had no protection from him whatsoever. There was nowhere for me to escape. I had a huge responsibility I was juggling. I was emotionally disturbed. I couldn't imagine I was even in this position. I thought I was a smart person. I had managed to escape bad relationships. I instantly avoided abuse and drama.

Vlad a narcissistic psychopath, was so convincing, so great at acting out his character. His parents were his trainers. They had lied and had proof to back their lies. They showed me pictures of Papa Vlad with mayor Dinkins in New York City. He explained he owned a real estate Magazine that was very popular. They even showed me copies of the magazine. One of Papa's most conniving pitches to me was when we got the equity money out, we would spend money on advertising for me. He would also create another Real Estate magazine to capture leads. We had a solid plan to generate more money. I even came up with a name for the magazine. *The Owner.*

I was beyond excited and kept thanking God for this blessing. I was sold a dream so big, I had to forgive myself. I was just a young girl with big dreams and very unfortunately met with a pack of demons in human clothing. That dream, in reality, was a house of cards that collapsed with the winds of the crash of 2008.

# NEW YEAR NEW TRAUMA

In January 2009, Vlad came over to bring me food. We opened a bottle of champagne to celebrate the New Year. Vlad initiated intimacy, we had not had any relations for months. It was not expected. I was broken and lost so I just let it happen. One month later I found out I was pregnant. I wanted to keep my baby. At almost forty, this could have represented my last best chance to conceive. Vlad reacted with rage, screaming me and threatening me if I kept the baby, he would make my life even more miserable. Now I knew for sure he never loved me and this was all a game to him.

I felt so abandoned and unworthy to live. I had to make the most heart wrenching decision of my life. I went into seclusion for two days. I prayed and prayed for the answer. In my heart, I already knew if I were to have this baby, I would fear for my life and be in a constant battle with Vlad. I would be tied to him and his family forever. I was so tired. Enduring those four years of mental and physical abuse left me weak and with no vision of my future. I could only see my immediate future, and it was not good. I was about to be homeless. I had no car, no solid job, and my body needed rest, both emotional and physical. I needed to be in a safe place.

I was a month into my pregnancy. I had a friend who drove me to the place, I cried and cried, and even at the last moment, I tried to stop the abortion. I just had no fight in me, no energy. I surrendered to God. What else could happen? How much more trauma could I endure?

# RETURNING HOME: BLOOD BETRAYAL

In 2011, my mom's condition was getting worse. She had COPD and was on oxygen 24/7. I realized I needed to go back to New Jersey to be with her. I moved from Florida to care for her. She specifically said I could not bring my cat Leo of thirteen years because she was allergic. I now had to let go of the only love I had go. I loved Leo more than words could describe.

Additionally, I had lost all of my friends due to my toxic relationship with Vlad. I was destitute and needed help. Vlad volunteered to watch Leo as he did love him and Leo knew him. I reluctantly agreed. Two months later, I received the news that Leo was missing. I never saw my Leo again. My heart was now shattered into trillions of pieces. I knew the end of me was near. How much more could a human take?

It was heartbreaking to see my mother's condition worsen. For six months, I did my best to care for her. I changed her diapers, fed and bathed her. I needed money so I began working in New York City as a realtor during the day. I got licensed in a week and started learning commercial Real Estate agent. I was being trained by one the best agents on the West Side. His name was Jerome Rock, who was Chris Rock's uncle. I was starting all over.

It kept my mind busy yet my nerves were so stressed to the breaking point. Taking the subway to show properties in the pouring rain, feet wet, cold air. I missed Florida so much. I even at times decided to sleep in the office basement. If it was too late, I did not want to take the subways or *NJ Path* train because it was very dangerous. Opting to sleep under a desk or the creepy basement was definitely safer.

I endured this for six months, and on February 12th, 2012, I got a phone call from my sister saying come home now. My cousin Lauren and I both worked in the city, so I met her at her job and we drove all the way to mom's house. The hospice nurses were there and they administered her death dose. I was so furious. They did not allow any last words to be spoken and my sisters will deny to this day they gave the orders. When we arrived, she was already unconscious, basically a morphine zombie.

I was crying hysterically and desperately trying to get a response from my mom. It was too late; I was too late. The shutting down of organs had begun. I was holding her hands and putting a wet sponge in her mouth to keep her hydrated. I went into shock immediately. I knew it because everything around me looked different, as if I was in a different dimension.

My body felt floaty and light as if I was plugged into some kind of frequency. It felt like a dream state, too. All I could do is wish this was not happening. I wanted to drift inside my mom and tell her I loved her. My mom, the person who gave me life. I flowed through her portal to get this precious gift from her. I never saw her this way, a portal to the Earth realm. It was surreal. To think this human form would be no more.

During my mother's death process, people started gathering in her living room. It was evening and we had all family members arriving, as well as her neighbors. My cousin Maria and my Uncle Franky arrived and immediately asked where was the priest? I was asked by my sisters to stay with mom while my sisters left to make all of the arrangements. I was so numb I did not even realize there was no priest. Maria frantically said we needed a priest! Without hesitation she called our Parish at St. Francis Xavier and, amazingly, a priest answered. He came quickly and recited the last rites and prayers. It was so perfect as my mom would have wanted. It was amazing to see so many neighbors show their love for her.

I particularly was moved to see the two Peruvian boys who lived down the street. My memory quickly went back to all the times she let them swim in our pool and made them lunch. It was so often; I would get upset with her. This one day I yelled her and said, "When are we going to get to use the pool?"

Geraldine looked me in the eye and said, "They were allowed any time they want and so are you.

I got pissed off and walked away. She loved giving to children. Almost every weekend she would go buy food and refreshments and have a barbeque inviting all the children on our block to our yard. This flashback made me realize my mother's heart was so beautiful. These boys showed up because she showed them love, kindness, and most of all, acceptance. It was an honor for them. I saw in their eye's deep sadness. I processed all of this in a delusional state. The last thing I recalled was holding my mom's hand and telling her I loved her.

The next thing I saw was two men coming in to take my mother away. I see a big black bag and I became conscious to realize what was about to happen. Like smelling salts, I jumped up and ran into the bathroom and four people followed. I could never see my mother in a body bag. I remember being put in one during my initiation into the North Ward Ambulance Squad. I was an EMT in training and passed the tests. The initiation included me being inside the zipped-up body bag, tied to the doors of the ambulance to be dragged around our neighborhood. It was horrible indeed.

My uncle Franky, Aunt Nancy, my cousin Maria, and I all agreed we could not fathom having this vision of her in a body bag. My uncle then asked why there was no priest and I could not answer him. I only said my sisters handled everything. What happened next was something I never imagined. The arrangements made for my mom were untraditional to say the least for a Catholic woman.

They would not have a mass or a viewing. All of the family members were upset and contacted me. I was the one who was always in communication. My sisters got wind of the questions and angst as everyone became irate. My older sister Selena actually came up to my face yelling at me. "I do not need you or anyone judging me. I don't need any of you and in fact, I disown you."

Her rant went on much longer but that was the gist. I have not spoken to her since 2012. She did not show up for the burial or the family dinner gathering. My younger sister showed up to the burial but not to the gathering. It was clear from that day, the hate and malice in their hearts for me and the extended family. I never knew they could be so callous. Learning that was very difficult.

The family gathering was beautiful. My cousin Jose cooked delicious food and we sat and talked about all the fun times we had with Geraldine. There was this strange occurrence that motivated me and I took action. The funeral card they chose was so random. As if they did not know or care who our mother was. I called up the funeral home and asked them If I could change the cards to something my mom would have wanted. They asked, "Who are you"?

I said, "I am her daughter Violet". It took them a moment to realize I existed and said yes. I was so excited to create this for her. My mom always wanted to be a singer and she would write little songs and share them with all of us in an email. I saved all of her writings, and this one was very beautiful. I feel her spirit inspired me to do this. This was the card's revision:

### The Lovely Sky

If you fall and a wing should break, call out to me and my heart you'll take
I'll set your wing so you can fly along with me in the lovely sky,
I will set your wing so you can fly in the lovely sky,
if you fall and two wings should break
still call to me and my heart you will take

I'll set your wings so you can fly along with me in the lovely sky
side by side just you and I, together we'll fly
Then we will fly to our nest, there I will love you the best

forget all of the rest
And then we will fly and fly, side by side
In the lovely sky, the lovely sky, in the lovely sky.

A day after the funeral, my two sisters came into my mom's apartment where I was living and started throwing everything out. I protested and asked them what was the rush? They had their flouting attitudes on, acting high and mighty, intent on discarding all of her contents.

I was flabbergasted as to why they were in such a rush. One day after her passing, all her belongings were being removed. They wanted none of it and thought all of her possessions were garbage. I was homeless and could not keep anything, but I knew family members wanted some things for keepsake and remembrance. My sisters basically said it all had to go. I called whomever to come get it now!

I felt as though I was in a race, stressed from the death of my mom and now having to save her beautiful things. She had saved things I made her from eighth grade. I am glad I was there or they would have thrown it out. In shop class, I made a wooden heart with an arrow going through it. I had etched the word "Mom" on it. It was polished and it was always on view for my mom. I actually buried it with her. I placed it in her hands in her coffin.

What came next is even more morbid. My sister threatened me and told me I could not stay there. She had plans to rent it out and needed me gone. She knew what I just went through and had not one caring bone in her body. It was as if she was waiting for this her entire life. She discarded me, not even letting me grieve for my mother. It was my house too, yet she knew she forced me off the deed and had total control. I basically realized this and the hurt was deep inside my broken heart. I was worth $800 to her. That was the rent she collected as I was homeless with a mountain of losses behind me.

This was the ultimate betrayal. Why? What did I do to deserve this? I still cannot believe my own blood would do this to me. Banned from my home at the worse economic time in my life. I was being punished for being different and that day changed my perspective on family forever. I never did anything to warrant this kind of hatred or disrespect. I turned to God for understanding and forgiveness. To take one step, to breathe one more breath was so difficult in the face of this treatment. I knew the Devil wanted me badly, to have the two people who supposedly loved me but ultimately turned against me. This was surely the work of dark forces. I meditated and was lifted up in spirit immediately. I leaned on my cousin Lauren until I got the message to where God wanted me next.

# EXILE: CALIFORNIA DREAMING TO LAS VEGAS PROSTITUTE

There is a saying, when you are broken or damaged, the wolves can sense this and come in for the kill. I do believe this because it is what surely happened to me. During my absolute worse time in my existence on this planet, I encountered many wolves posing as sheep. By this time in 2012, I had lost everything you can possibly lose in a life time, and all within four years. I lost my child, investments, my home, all finances, jewelry, credit, car, all friends, mother, my beloved cat Leo, my two sisters, my inheritance, and my most of all, trust in myself.

I was a shell of nothingness. I was confused, numb, and in shock. Following a sense, blindly looking for a rescue. It was so difficult to describe those feelings of utter decimation of character, mind, and soul. My body still worked thankfully. I had so many scars, both seen and unseen. I had no drive or desire to live or to create. I was on my knees praying for solace every lucid moment. I prayed for death to peacefully slip me away. It was as if were dead anyway. I did however, have a strong force holding me upward. An invisible hand gripping me, keeping me awake, and in tune to nature.

I knew from all of my previous experiences with God the powerful creator I was going to get through this someday. To have the patience to endure the *someday* was the gift given to me by God. I slipped in and out of other dimensions, surreal and beautiful yet excruciatingly painful. One uncanny thought was wherever I went, there was a white animal. I encountered Milkshake, a white West Highland Terrier. There was Tibet, a Tibetan Terrier. Another was Bigboy, a fluffy Persian. Finally, there was Boots, a Maltese.

I bonded with all of them on my journey and watched over them. Looking back now, they were my sherpas along the way. The love I gave to them was received and given right back. It kept my heart pumping, with a reason to keep living. What I thought was God giving me a hand to hold in my darkest hour, turned out to be a demonic force trying to seal my dark fate. I called a college friend from Montclair State University to ask her for advice. Veronica, her sister Lilian, and I had all graduated from Montclair State University. Veronica was the younger sister of my best friend and an attorney at law.

We had not spoken in over ten years but I knew she was practicing law in California. We spoke for a while and I told her about all of my losses and trauma. I asked her some legal questions as I was so lost as to how to recover from my misfortunes. I truly had no one to talk with or turn to. Veronica offered me a trip to California to take a step back and review options. She offered to pay for my flight and stay at her home. As she put it, she was in financial abundance. I looked around at my situation and thought, what else do I have? I am basically homeless with no immediate family or friends.

I thought it would be good for me as I did not like New Jersey and going back to Miami would keep me in a depression after all I had endured there. She booked me a one-way ticket on *Frontier Airlines*. I sat on the train to the airport in *Penn Station* with my two luggage's. I looked around and felt nothing. I had no hope, no desires. I was weak and apathetic. It was the most eerie feeling.

My memory of being on the plane is almost not existent and how I got to Veronica's home in Santa Monica, California. I arrived July 11, 2012. I vividly recalled walking up the driveway and to the left of the front door, there were beautiful large lavender and rosemary bushes. It was pleasant smelling and visually appealing. It calmed me and gave me a good vibration.

My position had begun as Veronicas personal assistant. I was to do whatever she needed. I started out doing little things like cooking and driving her to appointments. A week after being in Los Angeles, I was asked to drive her to her Las Vegas home. I drove her car 3.5 hours through the desert to and from Vegas. In Vegas, she spoke to me about her new job and her ventures she was starting. Her primary way of making money was being a stripper in Las Vegas. She told me she purchased her home with the money she made. I was in shock, as she was a shy, nerdy type in school. She increased her breasts to triple D so that gave her more confidence. She explained that being a lawyer got in the way of her true desire of being an actress. Stripping gave her access to money and time.

I was informed of my job description doing what she needed me to do. I drove her to and from work. I woke up at four AM or later when she called, I drove her home. I was shooting video and editing marketing material for a website she was developing. Six months into living with Veronica the unfathomable happened. She casually called me into the living room after speaking to someone on the phone.

She said a friend of hers was coming to town and he wanted a companion. She then said he was going to pay $1500. My eyes widened. "What is the $1500 for?" I knew by her face what was expected. Veronica said she would take $500 for a service fee. I was so insulted and enraged. I yelled at her and said, "No fucking way."

Then she said. "How do you think you will make it in this town with nothing"?

It hurt me so much to think I trusted this person with my healing after everything I have been through. All the loss and trauma, she wanted to take what was left of me, my integrity and innocence. Demonic overlay projected onto me. I stood my ground and vehemently refused.

The greatest thing that happened was she met a married man who was so wealthy, he was throwing so much money her way. Veronica was always going on trips with him. She needed me to take care of her home and dog. I was safe from madam pimping me out. We even moved into his six-million-dollar mansion her lover owned. We stayed there until the mansion was sold. It was a beautiful home in Chatsworth, California. Veronica asked me to come to Aspen with her to shoot a video. I told her I would work only for money! She offered me $500 and a paid trip. I agreed without hesitation.

I had my protective force field up around her. She saw my boundaries and did not cross them. I did what she asked and got to truly enjoy Aspen. We skied and ate lovely dinners at the *Regency Hotel*. I felt like royalty. I even charged massages to our room. We were staying in the hotel next to her lover. He booked us rooms while he and his wife and two children were next door. This was so disgusting. I had the task of filming them in the jacuzzi canoodling and kissing. I did what I needed to do to make money.

I recalled walking around Aspen at night alone just to feel the vibe. I walked into a theater and watched a movie with Leonardo DiCaprio. The streets were white and glistening. I felt as if I were in another world. We went to the famous Caribou Club and danced the night away. On our return from Aspen, to California, again I became the servant of course. It was a lovely six-bedroom estate with a waterfall pool and slide. Tennis courts, fruit trees, jogging path and beautiful fire places and enormous winding staircase.

I hardly recall being there. It is all is a bit blurry. She used it as an opportunity to hold model auditions for Angels, as she called it Angel Mansion. I took photos of the angel auditions and produced a huge party, which I personally catered for over fifty people. I had asked my musician friend from Miami to perform. It was an amazing party. We lived in it for six months before it sold.

Having to move back to Santa Monica bungalow was a drab. We continued to drive to Las Vegas every weekend. There was a business venture that came up and I began to take my power back. Her lover bought her a fourteen-seat limo bus to drive tourists around town. My friend Keith, who worked at the Casino as a time share manager, had lists of client leads. I negotiated a deal which gave me a decent percentage for transacting this deal. She immediately did not like the idea of me making more than her measly $200 a week. Veronica became very angry and did not like competition. I was to stay in my humble position or I would be cast out.

# GOD TO MY RESCUE

One very sizzling hot day in Las Vegas, Veronica and I got into a heated fight over the deal I negotiated. She was very aggressive with me and I did not like her attitude. I argued back, pushed her out of my room, and locked the door. She screamed through the door. My instinct was to grab my things and leave. Most of my things were in her California home. I had two big bags and luggage. I quickly grabbed my things and proceeded to walk out of the home. She came after me saying she was calling the police.

I laughed at her and headed down the street in mid-day 114-degree weather. Magically a truck with a couple in it drove passed me. I flagged them down. Minutes before our fight, my dear friend from Florida, Keith, called me to tell me he was in Vegas. I asked him which casino and he was around the corner from where I was located. I knew in my heart God had laid out the stones for me to step upon. This was just too perfect. The couple asked. "Where are you going?"

I answered. "*South Point Casino* please." I arrived and dragged my melted body and luggage into the casino. I went to the bar area in shock once again. Would I ever be safe again? It dawned on me in my broken state that I was prone to more abuse and trauma. It was like a strong magnet finding its way to me. Seemingly nice people or friends had turned on me, trying to further destroy me.

Keith however, was my lifeline. I always trusted him and I explained what had happened to me. I told him how vindictive Veronica was and she would probably keep all of my belongings. He then offered to rent me a car to drive to Santa Monica to get there before her and gather my things. I was so excited and filled with fear of the unknown. Would she be there? I was in a race for my life, for the little items I have left from my prior life.

I got the SUV rental and began my journey back to Los Angeles. Driving fast, my heart keeping time with the speed of the SUV. My mind ran various scenarios, fear combined with disappointment. My soul said. "You will not be defeated." When I arrive at the home the locks were changed. My key did not work, so I called to the other roommate but no one answered. Veronica must have called them and told them to lock me out. I started to cry as I could not get in.

My things in the yard were locked in a bin. I could not get inside. I called the police, told them, and they came rather quickly. They knocked on the door and no one answered. The police were informed someone must be home. They said to call again if someone came to the house.

I went to my car hysterically crying, thinking she had defeated me. She had won just, the all the others, like Vlad and his wretched family. All of these demons who had succeeded in fooling, deceiving, stealing, and abusing me. I cried and screamed so loud. All of sudden, I got the notion to look though my phone for help.

I scrolled down to a guy I briefly met on a date a few months earlier. His name was Mauricio. I called him and told him what just happened, and he said loud and clear. "Break in." My heart and mind could not accept his suggestion. I refused to follow his advice. He screamed. "Do you want your things?"

I said, "Yes!"

He said, "Break in and get what is yours now!" He actually gave me the courage. I went to the half open window, picked at the screen, and slowly peeled it out of its slot. As I lifted it up, I saw in the room a movement. It was Dave, our other roommate. He was slouched inside the closet hiding. I screamed at his to let me in, and he said no.

I jumped down and called the police again and told them someone was home. They came back to the home, called out his name, and he had no choice but to answer the door. The police asked him If I lived there and he said yes. The police stayed until I loaded up all of my things. Unfortunately, I could not fit two of my favorite paintings.

I drove away with a victory under my belt, the first one in a while. I screamed. "Victory!" A friend of a friend was subleasing a room and I took over his room. I paid $500 as a deposit, and moved all of my things inside.

My former abuser, Vlad made his way out to California to make sure I met his new Swedish model girlfriend. I kept getting salt in my wounds, impossible to heal or feel safe. Vlad helped me move my things inside this new apartment. I took each hit gracefully. I felt God's armor surround me and it softened the blows. Every time I looked at him, all I could think is you crazy, sick bastard look what you have done to me. I am homeless, destitute and broken, just where you wanted me. I wanted to defeat him; I still do. I want to win.

The best thing about the new apartment was it was close to Venice Beach. I felt safe there, as my roommate was a handsome young Aussie. He was very pleasant and nice to me. Living in Los Angeles, broken in pieces, seemed fitting to be around angels. I can definitely say it felt more devilish than angelic. I was given my best effort to survive, to heal and find a reason to live. I vividly recalled feeling so disconnected from the planet and my purpose. I just used my camera and my curiosity to stay sane and most importantly, live in the present moment.

The series of unfortunate events left me gripped by fear, distrust, confusion and deep sorrow. I had lost all the tangible and intangible things one could lose in a lifetime, all in a matter of a few years. How could this be possible? How could anyone survive the loss of all their hard work, fortune, credit, homes, car, cat, mother, child, siblings, and most of all, faith, AKA *trust*? I can attest it was a horrific journey, and so far, I had survived. I survived because of my mental strength. It was as if I was geared up for this my whole life. To endure and outsmart the darkness. I was victorious in many ways.

I was able to rise up from the ashes like the Phoenix. Each time the dark struck down on me, the escape path was laid out before me. My God and savior made no haste in his communication with me, as my channel was open to his words, his command. He saved me countless times and I still do not know why. Why would he save me each time? One would think the dark would stop haunting and taunting me, yet another attack was inflicted on me.

I prayed every second for it to stop hurting, the pain, the sorrow, the defeated spirit dragging me down. Even my physical appearance deteriorated from all the stress and abuse. I knew the only way out of it was through it. This was the ultimate and most difficult process of healing trauma. After leaving Las Vegas, I thought this has to be the end. I prayed my karma was complete and a trend of joy and restoration was on the horizon. How could a human take much more?

I now have no friends out here, no car and no credit. I was devastated and just did not fathom how I could survive here with no help. My only friend or support was God. I had to put complete faith in him and I did. I went back to the day on the train to the airport that eventually took me to California. I said to God. "I have given up my idea of my life as nothing has turned out good. I gave my life to you and I promise not to interfere or make a move without your consent."

By consent, God would have to physically move me into action toward the next stepping stone. I had completely surrendered my will and it felt great. I no longer had to make decisions or worry. Well, the only worry was, what will happen next? I never knew how things were going to turn out or get done. I was in for a surprise as things unfolded. It was like watching someone else's life movie. It got exciting at times, not knowing if this day would be my last day on Earth. I now saw my life like a game of chess or any game where someone else moved me around according to a higher plan I had forgot, or perhaps, I never knew the plan.

I am still not sure how it worked. Yet some clues of the important experiences tied into my childhood as if it had to happen. So partly I believed I was on my divine path surrendering my ego was necessary to complete my mission here on this planet. I was so desperate for help and it never seemed like I would ever get out of this black hole of nonexistence. While I tried not to be, I was in pure survival mode. I held composure each step and knew somehow, I would get by. No one could tell I was on the brink of homelessness every single day.

This one lonely day, I decided to take a bus to Main Street. I needed to explore and feel human again. I put on my maxi dress and a cool looking hat and started out on my way. I found myself at a bus stop bench waiting. Many people were waiting and I noticed a few musicians standing behind me. A dark-haired woman sat next to me and introduced herself as Fedra, the lead singer of the band standing behind us. I replied with my name and showed great interest in her band. I love music and bands as I managed a few musicians in Miami. She said their van broke down that day, which is why they were waiting for a bus.

She quickly shared her artistic vision she had for the video of their new song. I called this a crazy miracle moment. It was definitely divine. Had their van been working, we would never have met. I immediately told her I could produce their video. We exchanged numbers and planned to meet again to further discuss the video. Their bus came and left, and I remained seated on the bench wondering what just happened? I just became a video producer for a band relying on me. I did not even have a camera, let alone any other equipment for video production. I went to main street walked around and had lunch. "Fake it till you make it" is a saying, and I knew God would provide. I knew this experience was pre-ordained. I did not have any clue how this would all come to fruition. I followed every clue God gave and stepped on each stone placed before me.

I called a friend I had met in New York City who was now living in Las Vegas. I did a photoshoot with him a few years prior. I asked him to come to Los Angeles to shoot this video. We had no money to offer of any kind. As unbelievable as it sounds, he said yes! He even brought an assistant director and producer with him. The actors were all Los Angeles based talent and friends of the band. Fedra was the lead singer, wrote the script, and hired all of the actors while I added a few. I purchased food and beverages for the cast and crew. I even filmed two scenes and appeared in two.

The production went smoothly and it came out as good as can be expected with no budget. To this day, I am very proud to have been a part of it. *The Moon is Shining in Your Eyes* by *Skygazers*. It was a truly fun and artistic experience. I was in my zombie state performing and producing, yet not being fully there. I was in a split off realm. The one realm where I was destitute, broken, sad, shocked, and numb and the other was where I was in action, doing what was necessary to survive and pretend not be in survival mode.

It was so confusing and all I could do was stay in the present, as I focused on the task at hand. Many have undergone this type of mind-altering dystopia. I know I did my best and I was guided by someone, something divine. They gave me the little bit of hope nuggets, just to stay alive and feel human. I prayed for miracles for God to take me to him immediately. I wanted no part of this disgusting feeling. I never knew it could exist inside me. To be a zombie and human at the same time is a phenomenon that no words to describe.

As if the demonic Vlad did not do enough to break my soul, he came up with a way to try to finish me off. He tried the very last time to shatter my confidence even more than he had already done. He did the unthinkable and at one moment, I thought I would die. I actually thought my soul would explode into a million pieces and be transported back to my galactic home. I was now living in a shared apartment in Venice Beach, California. I was so alone, frightened, and just not equipped with all my bearings, energy, and confidence. I did not know where to go or what to do with myself. I relied on God to direct me.

I received a call from my abuser Vlad. He lured me in with taking me to lunch and I somehow wanted him to give me money – the money he and his father stole from me. I needed to survive out there, and I needed money. I should have known his real reason to come to California, yet I was in the darkness of my own pity. I asked him for money and he said no. I cried and got more upset. "Why are you out here following me? Leave me alone!"

I remember getting into a fight, so surreal yet again. I moved all the way across the state lines to get away from this creep and he returned. He dropped me off and told me he was going to the annual Halloween

Party on Hollywood Boulevard, and asked if I wanted to join me and his girlfriend. I was about burst into tears, yet my solemn soul could not even cry one more tear for this insensitive, abusing asshole. He began to describe Jasmine, his twenty-two-year-old Swedish model from Miami. I was seated next to him, staring as if to say. "Why do you insist on trying to decimate me, my soul, my kindness, my joy?"

I knew then he was truly and deeply a sick man with more than just demonic tendencies. He was a destroyer of light a destroyer of confidence, love, trust, and compassion. Something grew inside of me and it was powerful. One side of me felt shame, disgust, envy, jealousy, and self-loathing. I wanted to run away and hide under a rock. He made me feel as though I was old, disgusting, a throw away, used up skin bag of a woman. He took all I had to give and left me to die in Miami. Now he was here to finish me off.

All of a sudden, the other side grew powerful and strong and my confidence grew to ten feet tall. I actually had the idea to tell him yes, I would go with them to the party. I felt absolutely crazy but I did it, I said. "Yes, pick me up." I knew God was up to something. I went to my little room picking through luggage to find a costume dress, anything that would make me feel beautiful. I knew a Swedish model twenty-five years my junior would be absolutely gorgeous, yet this was my time to shine in the face of this fear of agism.

God gave me the strength and confidence. I was shaking uncontrollably and my mind was set to listen to my guides, as I was not able to handle this situation alone. I got into the car and I saw her youthful beautiful face and long blond hair. My stomach turned into little knots. I was in the back seat quietly trying to listen and feel my way. I recalled small talk and not much details. We went to dinner and since I was vegetarian, I would always like to eat Pho soup. Vlad knew this and specifically took me there.

Jasmine wanted to get something else to eat and she got up and left the table. She was gone for a while. I continued to eat even though each spoonful I gagged, although he never knew the level of my discomfort. This was my greatest performance to date. My stomach was in knots, and she was in distress, as well. He made this the most uncomfortable evening for everyone. I drew upon my past acting skills and exhibited extreme confidence.

I looked good too, my breasts were busting out of my gold and pink sequined bandeau dress, and, of course, she was not very well endowed. My long, leggy, 5'7 frame was enhanced by black high heels that evening. In my weakened frame of mind, I almost forgot I still had very attractive assets as a mature woman. I should describe Jasmine's costume, also. She was truly a beautiful girl. The legs on Jasmine were just wow! She was a very long-legged police woman. How ironic, she could have arrested this abusing crook that stole not only from me, but from a handful of women both prior to me and after me. Would she be his true love, the one he would cherish and take care of? I don't know.

All the black eyes he gave me and other women. He actually dated a woman whom was older than me after we were together, and punched in her face. That was the thanks she got for buying him a *Bentley* and *Lamborghini*.

We found a parking spot and began to walk along Hollywood Boulevard. It was a fun experience as I loved the energy of the people and the costumes. I kept my upbeat energy and confidence as I walked behind the two love birds holding hands. We walked by many establishments and this one was playing the most amazing house music. I immediately walked in and started dancing. Dancing always gives me confidence and high frequency vibes.

I pretended to like Vlad for the sake of the night and my balance. I began dancing and he danced with me. We enjoyed each other for a few moments. Jasmine looked on with a blank stare. I just kept laughing, smiling, and feeling free for the moment from all of my shame, sadness, suppression, and depression. This man dancing in front of my face had taken everything from me. He even tried to kill me several times and I laughed as if I was nothing. I became a psychopath that evening.

I wanted so badly to pull her to the side and scream *run*! I feel bad to this day I did not. The thing about psychopaths is they try to get past partners to corroborate they are good people. He was being nice, buying me dinner when her knew he robbed my whole life from me and knowing my desperation, I would go along with his plan. I should have screamed at the top of my lungs, for all to hear. "Vlad is a *psychopath*!" I am sure like he had done many times before, accusing me of being crazy to all of the new people in his life. He and his father told the police each time I called them, I acted crazy because I was on my period. Gaslighting, Vlad's favorite tactic.

One Miami Beach Police officer agreed. "My wife does the same thing." I knew what I was up against and it was too late for Jasmine. She was in his clutches under mind control. I prayed for her that night she would be released from his grip. The night ended and we headed back to where he was staying and we were all tipsy. I recalled staying in the car until he sobered up. There was dead silence, as I felt nothing for this blob of human feces.

He expressed that Jasmine was upset. I assumed I had rattled her soul, as they fought because she said to him. "What is she on? She is doing some kind of drugs!" Vlad stood up for me, as he knew I did not do drugs. I just get high on music and dance and let out my true essence. He told her she did not do drugs and he later said she could not understand the freedom I expressed without doing drugs. Jasmine was very jealous of how we connected and danced together. He told her it comes with maturity! I could hardly believe how I turned this trauma around. It was then, I realized why I had to go out with these two idiots.

God did not disappoint me, as I was vindicated and released from any further trauma. I knew what he had to contend with and was happy to know he would have to suffer as much as I did. She was ten years younger than him and he would have to pay the price. I never saw Vlad again. He is now married and had a child with Jasmine, and I know nothing of their life together. I blocked all of their social media profiles.

I was faced with another setback. The roommate I was subleased from in Venice Beach was returning. I had to move, yet again. I was waiting for my next stepping stone. I prayed for a safe solution as always. I had kept in touch with the band *Skygazers*, as we were still editing our music video and planning the release party. I got the notion to ask them if I could crash at their place.

They agreed to let me stay temporarily. This would be my next stone AKA – home. I moved in to their studio with them. I was so relieved I was not alone anymore. I felt connected with creative people and safe in a new city. I recalled creating music videos and hosting a video release party at a swanky Los Angeles restaurant on Pico Boulevard. We created great things together. It didn't end so well as I got into an altercation with Fedra's husband.

I left immediately and moved down the hall from them. The building was originally an office building. It was very creepy and the bathrooms were down the hall. There were no showers, just a raggedy bathroom. I recalled having to brush my teeth in the gross sink. There was a neighbor to whom I was introduced across the hall. His name was John. He had introduced me to his friends, Jennifer and a guy named Ritchie. There was also a yoga studio across the way and we all took classes there. I felt very uncomfortable living there since the vibe was negative between me and Fedra's husband. I wanted out of there quickly. I prayed to God to elevate me to safety.

# ENTER THE DIAMOND

A friend of mine I knew from Miami, contacted me and had invited me to lunch at the *Soho House* on Sunset Boulevard. He asked me what I had been doing on the west coast and I told him I was making videos. The awful reality was I was homeless and living in an abandoned office building with a musician couple. I could only laugh and cry, as he met me at my beautiful home in South Beach at a dinner prepared by my Greek friends. I was once thriving and now was surviving as a fraud. Yet I rose the occasion. I showed him the music video I produced.

He said, "How cool. I have a friend who is making a movie out here, perhaps you should speak with him?" He gave me the number and was so excited inside. I was seeking my next stepping stone. God did not disappoint. Divine timing and coordination of all the necessary players.

I called Bob, the director, and introduced myself. We made a date to meet to discuss the details. We met at a coffee shop in Brentwood called *Coral Tree*. He was seeking a second Director of Photography. I told him I was available. The position was for credits only. Shooting began in 2013 and wrapped in 2016. It was the most amazing experience, with incredible people. I loved the experience and the cast holds a special place in my heart.

www.enterthediamond.com

The significance of this happening was so divine as I finally made it to Hollywood! I worked on a movie and actually received credit as a cinematographer. I finally got my desire and it was more amazing than I imagined. I hope my mom and dad saw my little accomplishment in Hollywood. Some people go to Hollywood and try for years to get a credit. It was all in my divine plan.

I found a shared apartment/room on Sepulveda Boulevard for $500. I just needed to move my things. I had to ask my friend Ritchie to lend me his car. He insisted I come by his friend James's house. I recalled a guy flailing his arms up and down to guide me into a parking space. He lived on Venice Boulevard. I parked the car and made my way inside the apartment. James, Ritchie, and a woman were inside. I came in and said hello to everyone. There was a beautiful white fluffy Persain kitty name Big Boy. I felt at ease and was able to finally relax. I was handling way too much stress.

James was a musician, a guitarist to be exact. They were listening to music and practicing as a band when I arrived. I just listened and enjoyed the collaboration. James did have a very strong appeal. He was tall, confident, sexy, and handsome. I liked him and felt a magnetic pull towards him. James sent secure messages he was interested and it felt nice to have a connection.

James invited me to a Fourth of July party. I got into his car and I felt some kind of metaphysical shift. It was a nice home filled with lots of people. We were having so much fun together. We laughed and felt the vibes that were amazing. I had not felt anything good for so long. I needed this connection to prove I was still alive. My atoms perked up, my soul was interested, and for a moment, I was out of my survival and self-pity mode.

Love was the source of my troubles. It made me very hesitant to feel that again. It was so organic. +I had no choice but to accept it and let it flow. We explored the house and found a table with an Asian Drum Gong on it. I picked up the bow and struck it, the sound vibrated through both of us. It was as if we opened up a portal. After that gong things between us became magical.

# SCORPION STING WITH A TOUCH OF MAGIC

Do you believe in a Magic? I do! I have experienced throughout my life magical moments. I feel lucky in that respect. I guess you really do have to take the good with the horrible. On the third day of us being together with James, all was flowing naturally. I was so frightened to be hurt again. I knew at this point it was not up to me to fear anything as God had the control. I allowed what felt good to continue and if it did not feel good, I would be gone. That much is all I knew.

On the Fifth of July, something unexplainable happened between us. We were outside on his deck kissing and holding each other looking at the stars. He rolled on top of me and I knew what was going to happen. I felt it every cell saying yes! We stared at one another and we tilted our heads back and forth. I am not sure what I saw, but he realized it first. James exclaimed. "You look like you are twenty years old again! You just transformed in front of my eyes."

I screamed. "Oh my God! You too?" I could not believe it! He looked like a young boy. We shaped shifted into another time and space and we made love under the stars softly and gently staring at each other. While this was happening, there was a bubble or a force field shielding us. We both were in awe of this experience. It was divine and so pure.

We fell in love that night and I moved into his apartment. We were in bliss and it was healing my broken soul. We were in sync on many levels. We would work out at the gym together and go to Venice Beach. This unexpected love was just what I needed but I knew not what was about to come.

I recalled taking him to my favorite place to celebrate our one-month anniversary. Our celebration of canoodling and kissing filled my heart. Labor Day weekend, we were invited to a beach party. James's energy was not right, he acted differently. I knew something was off. I saw this woman staring at James. I found out later she was his ex-girlfriend from fourteen years ago. I did not know what trickery was unfolding behind my back. It turned out Ritchie was his henchman, collecting women for him.

I thought. "Dear Lord not again, another demon trying to destroy me?" As broken as I was, how was I going to deal with this? From what I gathered; James had been trying to connect with his ex-girlfriend Natalie for months on *Facebook* before meeting me. He could not get her to answer his messages. He then employed Ritchie to become friends with her on *Facebook* and invited her to the party where we were invited. She responded and showed up to the party. Once she saw him, she was set on getting him back, as they had an abrupt breakup and never spoke again – until that night. We began fighting and I moved out by November 2013.

I made a quick getaway and proceeded to heal once again from betrayal. I was desperately trying to stay faithful to God. My heart was severely broken and my mind confused. I did not understand this torture. I really wanted to die on Valentine's Day, 2014. I could not help but believe I was destined for. My aura was damaged and I was the feast of the demons. Taking blow after blow, bleeding from my soul, could I survive this? I was determined and I had to see this through.

I recalled screaming on the 405 freeway at the top of my lungs. "God, please send me help. I need help, please." I was floating around like a paper bag. I had no home, no real friends, no direction, or desires. It was so difficult. Such a stark difference from the life I had prior. I was driving on the 405 and the car in front of me had the license plate letters *Finch*, James's last name. I felt a knife slice me open and began screaming bloody murder to God. "Help me! Help me! *God*! *Why*? Help me please!"

I was broken once again. I was betrayed again! How could one human contain all of this pain? How could I endure much more? It felt as though my heart was in a meat grinder and each turn minced my soul. I was so numb. God knew I was about to break and perhaps this would be my last conscious moment. I wanted to leave my body. I was so very close to giving in to the dark.

Miraculously I get a message from *Plenty of Fish*, a guy named Scott had written to me. I replied and we began chatting. He lived in Hollywood and I lived in Culver City. He asked me out on a date and I said yes. He came to pick me up and we had dinner nearby. He was very handsome and tall, about 6'2". He was very funny, yet I could not laugh. I guess he picked up on my deep sadness and asked me what happened in my life to make me feel the way I did.

I burst into tears and began shaking with pain. He reached over and grabbed my hand to comfort me. After dinner, we walked and he held my hand. I was so numb; I could not even feel anything. I did not trust him yet, I had no one. He could have been a killer, but perhaps I just was so desperate to live. From that night, he wanted to be in a relationship. I took my time, reluctant to trust another person. He invited me out one night and I declined as I was very tired.

I was then awoken by a person jumping through my window. It was Scott checking on me to see if I was lying. Apparently, he had been with a lying cheater before me. I thought this was quite amusing, as I never had anyone mistrust me. It made me feel relaxed enough to trust him. We were then able to start on an even basis. I knew he at least was not a cheater, for he did not like how it made him feel.

After only a few weeks dating, he came to see the inside of my apartment. There was a lady named Diane living in the living room on a mattress. The other room was rented by a man named Ivan. I had a tiny room with a window facing the back of the complex. Scott was disgusted by the apartment and quickly decided I didn't belong there.

He told me I deserved better than this and wanted me to move in with him in his two-bedroom apartment in Hollywood.

I was shocked and not sure of anything as I was just a broken human. It felt so great to be loved and cared for and most of all respected. I told him I couldn't leave, however. I had signed a contract. Scott planned my great escape. One night he came with his big truck and we removed all of my belongings through the bay window and drove off into the sunset to Hollywood. He was an actor who procured decent roles.

I went with him to one of his filming's and had a blast. I began to feel again. He treated me so wonderfully. He gave me money and took me out to beautiful dinners. I cooked almost every day as well. We made music together. Scott wrote the story of my life in a song called *Black Sheep*. we co-wrote the lyrics and he wrote the music. It is so beautiful; I tear up every time I hear it, it marks my painful journey.

Scott made me laugh so hard that my pain took a back seat. I had a life where I could be proud. I was hired as a Director of Education for a learning center. I bought a *Mac* computer to store all of my photos. I bought a car for the first time in five years. I was truly getting my life back in order. I knew God sent me this man to get out of the clutches of the demons. I was still terribly damaged, but my soul wanted to thrive and be alive. I followed the path and listened to every message God had for me. We stayed together for a year and half, until it was time to continue on my journey. We ended as friends and I have fond memories of our time together.

Black Sheep Song by Scott Lee and Violet Light

Black Sheep Drifting alone at sea
Is your life what you thought it would be
Having to cross the state lines
Leaving your past behind
Water was thicker than blood
Wiped out your labor of love
All your dreams they stole
Now out West digging for Gold

A cry to heaven I came
Stubborn's your middle name
Your life will never be the same
But for the best
When I take your hand into mine, why do you run away?

Red bull charging ahead with new horns
Feels so good to be reborn
Shedding all that old skin
Now it's your turn to win

Pushing your way to the top
Nothing will get you to stop
Not even bruises from the ride
Will you get out alive?

A cry to heaven I came
Stubborn's your middle name
Your life will never be the same
But for the best
When I take your hand into mine, why do you run away?

# CRENSHAW ATTACK

In 2015 I was an *Uber* driver at night to make money while filming during the day. One night, I was on my last call around ten PM. I realized I was far from my West Hollywood area. I was led to an area called Crenshaw. I instantly knew I should head back, but the final ride was a female passenger. I figured she would be my last and I would head back. I picked up Muhamadeena. I had difficulty finding her shop. She called me, and I finally found her. I picked her up from a hair salon. I smiled, said hello, and started driving. I noticed she did not put in her coordinates needed for where she needed to be dropped off. I looked in my rear-view mirror and asked her nicely, to type in the address.

She quickly replied. "I will tell you where to go." An uneasy feeling immediately grew in the pit of my stomach. My instinct said to ask her again. I did so, and this time she told me. "Shut the fuck up and drive." I slammed on my breaks and told her to get the fuck out of my car. I pulled over at a vacant gas station, she got out and headed away from my car.

I looked at my brand-new backseat, and saw she had spilled her soda. I jump out and got a towel from the trunk and began to dry the seat. I totally forgot to clock her out, so she came back screaming at me. "Clock me out so I can get another *Uber*!"

I got out of my backseat, looked her in her face, and said, "I would have but you spilled your soda all over my seat."

I cautiously backed up and went to open my driver door. I never thought to turn my back to her, but I had to, in order to open my door. My thought was she would not dare attack me because she was in the system and that would be a very ballsy move. As soon as I turned to open the door, she attacked me. That wretched scumbag grabbed my long hair in her fist, wound it up and with all of her weight, threw me to the ground. She lifted my legs off the ground, and I landed on my right elbow, crashing my hip into the concrete.

I was in complete shock, yet I quickly rolled over on my back, lifted my legs, and began kicking her with all of my power. My legs were moving faster than I could see. I felt as though I was getting help from the matrix. I wore riding boots with thick, one-inch heels. I was driving my heals into her hands, thighs, and vagina. She was desperately trying to mount me. I would not let that happen. I kept kicking and even tried to pull her down to the ground by grabbing her bag strap. The strap broke and her bag fell to the ground.

She tried to mount me from side to side. I felt as helpless as a turtle on its back, but kept shifting and kept kicking her. She screamed for me to stop kicking and countered. "I will stop when you back the fuck up"!" Our eyes locked, foam coming out of my mouth, and my promise to her was when I got up, I was going to kill her. She finally could not take it anymore and backed up. I then rocked my legs over my head and jumped up like a ninja. I landed on my two feet with my fists up in air.

I then told her she was going to pay for what she did. I was about to lunge toward her, but she backed up and pointed her bruised finger towards me, saying. "You better just clock me out." She ran around my car and disappeared into the darkness. I was in complete shock. I survived this attack while on my back. I recalled heading to James's house to wash my wounds. I called the police and *Uber* to report her. Dear lord, why did this happen? How lucky can one be? She could have had a knife or a gun. I almost died, yet I was spared again.

# LONGBEACH ADVENTURES

I was hired to do a photoshoot of a client that found me on *Facebook*. We had become friends instantly. The photoshoot was beyond what I thought I could do. For Kim, it gave her a new lease on her life. A divorcee after seventeen years in a verbally abusive marriage, her esteem was so low. She saw the photoshoot I did of her friend Jennifer that she had posted on Facebook. When we spoke, I told her I would shoot 3 different looks for her. Her assignment was to find three looks that spoke to her soul.

We then set a date and it was truly a magically shoot. Kim was ready to shed her sorrow and self-hate and wrap her new persona around her. After moving out of Scott's apartment, Kim offered for me to stay at her place in Long beach, California. She had two bedrooms. One was her son's bedroom, but he was gone every other week. I agreed and paid her rent. It was such a comfort to be with a friend. We went out dancing and met new people.

We went to art galleries and celebrated birthdays and holidays together. I then decided to do a short documentary of her life. Kim was so expressive and could light up a room with her energy. I knew she would be perfect to act in her own documentary. She agreed and we began filming. I recreated a snippet from her life as a single mom, going back to school to get her Masters while navigating the strange online dating scene through apps.

I was intrigued to see her determination to create a life she loved. There were very dark times as she met a man who became a stalker and she had to have him arrested. I captured exactly what she endured. The short is called *Blue Moon*.

# RETURN TO PARADISE

During a deep meditation, I received the message it was time to return to my home, Florida. I tried living in practically every major city in California and could not find the home feeling I had while in Florida. I believed I was healed enough to face any triggers or reminders of what took place. I was excited with a touch of fear. I knew it was the right path.

I loaded up my *Fiat 500* with all of my belongings and headed east. The drive from California to Florida was so amazing. I stopped in New Mexico to see the White Sands and I camped there overnight. White Sands was truly a breathtaking view! Imagine seeing white sun-glistening sand sparkling as far as the eyes could see. It was a dreamlike scene. I ran up and down, left and right, and rolled around and down the hills in the pristine white powder. I even threw myself into the sand because it called to me. I was so stunned that this existed and I realized once again the magnificence of Earth.

Sunset had just begun when I arrived at the camping site. I focused on putting up my tent and settling in. I had decided that I was going to burn all of Vlad's photos at the site. I carried them with me throughout for some reason. This would be a ritual to seal the fact that my past must stay in the past. Burning the pictures, watching the flames take away those little memories that were left behind in my mind. I could not do this before as I was not ready. I truly wanted to return to Florida renewed, ready to live my true destiny.

Healing from abuse and trauma is a beautiful but daunting process. After the burning ritual, I walked toward my tent and when I looked up into the sky, I stopped in my tracks. I gasped and stood frozen as if someone shot me with a stun gun. My jaw remained open in awe for what seemed an eternity. My eyes never saw such a sight. I reached out with both of my arms to the sky, trying to touch the twinkling stars. They seemed so close I could actually reach them. The blackest sky with the brightest lights, all close together. I was mesmerized to see millions of stars blinking in and out. What a vast universe, it made me understand astronomers' attraction for the stars.

Where have I been living? Under a polluted skyline in Newark. I regretted even more growing up in a big city. I missed all these years of seeing this incredible light show. I settled down in my tent that had an open view to the sky and I cried myself to sleep. God, nature, and me were perfect together. I felt so much love in my heart. I got on the road with a renewed sense of faith, love and inspiration. God was with me keeping me safe on my journey home.

I spoke with my friend Kim Bolognese, and she informed me she was living in Fort Lauderdale. We had not spoken since she was pregnant and moved out of our home. She was now divorced and was raising her son Stephen alone. She invited me to stay at her home upon my return. My intention was to reinstate my real estate license and began to build my business again.

I was so excited to rekindle our friendship. I arrived at Kim's home in Florida September of 2016 safe and sound. I met her son Stephen, who was all grown up. The last time I saw him he was only eight years old. A twenty-year old man was before me. I gave them both a big hug. We made dinner together and chatted all night.

We spoke about my adventures in California and our fond memories. We had so much history together. Kim and I would go out dancing six days a week together in New York City and New Jersey. We had so many great memories and laughs. Going back to our days of dancing in NYC till the sun came up was nostalgic. The different phases of a person's life are a privilege that some do not experience.

I gave them both a big hug. We made dinner together and chatted all night. We spoke about my adventures in California and our fond memories.

All was going well until one night, Kim and her son were having an altercation and it became slightly violent. Her son punched a hole in the bedroom door. He was behaving erratic and out of control. I walked outside as to not intervene. I presumed she had been dealing with this for a while. Later that night, we spoke and I told her I was sorry to hear she had been experiencing these altercations. She disclosed he was currently diagnosed with bi-polar disorder. I knew this would not be a suitable to stay.

# ARTHUR MY LOVE

I went to the beach the next day and sat and stared at the aqua blue liquid swishing back and forth. The breeze was so warm, just like it had always been. I had dreamed of Florida for so long. I lived in California for four years and only went into the ocean three times. The waters along the west coast are so cold and turbulent, you can look but not touch it. I love swimming in the ocean.

After my long swim, I looked online for a rental. I found a place close to Kim's home, so I called the number. A gentleman named Arthur answered. He had a sweet and loving voice. I told him I wanted to rent his room. His pleasant demeanor made me feel safe. I made an appointment to meet him the following day at eleven AM.

I arrived on November 17, 2016 at 11:00am, and I knocked on the door. I was greeted by a sweet warm eyed man with a big smile. He was in his 80's, but his energy appeared so much younger. I introduced myself and he walked me in to show me the room for rent. I loved the room as it was clean and had a big window with lots of sunlight. I said I will take it! I finally had a safe place to rebuild myself and my career.

Years went by and Arthur and I had created a remarkable friendship. His humor and stable mindset were a perfect match for me. I was a great support as he lived alone and did not like to be in solitude. All of his children were living their lives and he was left alone.

The relationship that formed between Arthur and I was so special and so needed for my healing journey. I knew my journey led me here for his healing too. I found out his story and just felt so much respect for this human. He told me everything that led him to this very moment. Arthur was born in New Hampshire. He married Shirley, his high school sweetheart and they had six children together. Arthur moved his family to Florida in the 1970's. He and Shirley inevitably divorced and he remarried a gold-digging Nicaraguan woman, who he later divorced. Arthur said after his second divorce, he was very depressed and suicidal.

He explained God gave him a second chance at life when a young women named Jude, whom was renting a room, became pregnant. She came to him and asked for his advice, as she did not want the child and thought of getting an abortion. He said a fire was lit in him and he pleaded with her not to abort the baby. He told her he would help her raise the baby. She told him she did not want to be a mom.

Arthur then declared he would adopt him and be his father. Arthur cried and begged her to let hm adopt her baby. Jude agreed, and she birthed a son named Austin. Arthur said it was the happiest he had been his whole life. He explained in the early days of fatherhood, he was busy working, building businesses and just not involved with raising his own children. He was just a provider, not a father. Arthur wanted to experience being a dad.

It was a beautiful story, as he claimed that Austin saved him from self-destruction. I loved this man and his stories, I wanted to know everything about him. He was from the same generation as my father. I felt a strong similarity between the two men. Their demeanor and mentality were both the same. Arthur brought Carmine, my dad to life again. I began to think how would my dad be at eighty-six years old? How would we get along?

I missed so much about him, I really wanted to have a relationship with my dad. I saw this as a chance to create a relationship with an elder I never had. I never knew my grandparents, as they died when I was very young. I never had any input from ancestors or elders. I had been navigating the matrix alone. God has always stepped in to be my invisible guide. I was so grateful for His wisdom.

On September 10, 2017 hurricane Irma hit the coast of Florida. We were left without power for almost eight days. I was worried about Arthur, as he was frail and the heat was unbearable. No one came to visit, not one of his family members.

Another pivotal moment we shared was when he discovered his daughter Christine was dying of cancer. She lived in Deland, Florida which is four hours North of Fort Lauderdale. He wanted to go see her, and asked me to go with him. I drove with him and we stayed at her home. It was a very sad moment in his life. He always described her as the sweetest daughter out of his four girls. She was indeed so loving, and at fifty-five to die of cancer was so horrible.

Chrissy just retired and was enjoying her life with her husband and two dogs. It was a heartbreaking experience. Arthur wished it were him instead of her. We drove up together again for her funeral. I was by his side and I know I gave him strength. Whenever he needed me, I was there.

I started studying for my real estate exam and any free time I had, I spent it with Arthur. During the day he was always busy in the yard cutting grass or tinkering in his tool sheds. I finally passed my test and we celebrated! He was so thoughtful and kind, just like I imagined my dad. One day, I was upset about something and cried in my room. I heard the door open. Arthur came in and patted my head. He said., "Don't cry, everything will be alright." It was the first time I felt this kind of fatherly love in a long time.

Our friendship grew stronger and stronger each day that passed. At times, I felt the feeling as if something would go wrong due to my past trauma. I feared he would betray me somehow. I lived with that horrible feeling every day. Over and over Arthur proved to be a loyal friend. We would have fights and immediately, we would apologize to each other. I found this love so endearing as I never knew it existed. My childhood was filled with disrespect and disregard of others feelings.

I signed with a real estate broker that supplied leads and I began to make sales. I sold $1,400,000 in my first year back. I felt empowered and back on track. I was getting my life back in a new and improved version. I also dove in learning how to detox the human body. I studied many medical journals and watched documentaries on top holistic doctors. I was determined to improve my health in mind, body and spirit. The discoveries lead me to becoming Vegan. I wanted to raise my vibration by healing all the parts that were broken. I even had the courage to reach out to my younger sister to mend our relationship. Damiana answered and I told her I was back in Florida and wanted to get to know my niece and nephew. She was very open and we began to communicate on video and in person. Everything was falling into place and I was getting back the important people in my life. I felt so much and it was healing all the broken parts of me. I went to NJ for the holidays and had the time of my life. My niece and nephew gave me so much love and acceptance.

# FINAL BLOOD BETRAYAL

In my heart I was very hurt that she nor my older sister did not try to contact me. They did not care about me or my life. They had disowned me, as if I did not exist. I was so devastated that my family could do this. I did not want to mention the past so I moved forward and stayed in the present.

Damiana was willing to reconnect and we began with a clean slate. I enjoyed chatting with her, and my niece and nephew. I went often to New Jersey to visit them several times and she even met me in New York City for my fiftieth birthday dinner. It was nice having family again. I love my niece and nephew so much; we had such beautiful times together. We played and laughed and exchanged cute gifts of love.

My faith was stronger than ever before. However, I needed to work on my esteem and confidence.

I began going to the beach and gym every day. I was determined to reclaim the life I had before Vlad. My mind, body, and soul needed to be aligned again. I was speaking regularly with my sister and the kids. I felt as though I had family and it lifted my soul. I spoke to my niece and nephew every day on video chat and visited often. My trust in life started to come back.

One day, Damiana expressed her desire to sell our family home. Since I am a realtor, I began sending her Customer Market Analysis and sales of homes in the area. I called a few realtors to see about listing the home. However, Damiana's husband quietly decided I could not be the realtor and hired another realtor. I also discovered they had rented my mom's apartment and began collecting the rent on three apartments with a rough estimate of $3400 per month for ten years, a whopping $408,000 in rental income, minus expenses.

It came time for me to ask her the question I had been holding inside me for ten years. I asked her how she would divide the inheritance with smugness. She said, "I get 50% and you will get 1/3 of our mothers 50%."

I spoke very softly and added, "I am a third owner of our home."

She quickly said. "No, you are not! You signed your name off the deed."

I said, "Yes, but not to lose my proceeds." I simply reminded her the only reason I signed my name off the deed was to calm her and my mother down and their false fears of the home being taken due to my possible foreclosures of my properties in Florida. I reminded her it was for protecting the property only and not to sign my share away. She quickly got angry and called me names ridiculing me.

I then realized I was scammed by her and her husband out of my inheritance. Her reason was I was living in Miami, and I did not deserve it. She declared she was the one managing the rentals and repairs. I explained to her she could get paid for management fees but I should still be owed part of the rental income and 1/3 of the proceeds of the sale.

In the pursuit of greed, Damiana, my younger sister, stole my inheritance and disowned me. This was the last communication from my sister. Lying and using derogatory language to hide her deceitful ways. I have emails of her pleading me to sign the papers she had from the attorney. Why would you remove a sibling from their inheritance, if not for monetary gain? It is very clear to anyone. What she and her husband did was all for monetary gain. The proof is in their bank accounts. I only hope she evolves and rethinks her actions.

Here are two of her emails. "I am cracking up over your behavior but anyway get your facts straight let's see, I did not force you off of the deed, mommy wanted you to come off. I have the agreement that is signed by you. I am sad for your sorry sick ass, you are unbelievable." And "You want more than you deserve"?

I have asked God over and over why do you and everyone forsake me? Why was I ostracized, betrayed, condemned, ridiculed and discarded? I could not understand how this happened? There is no love there, no compassion, and certainly no familial bond. I have pondered on what I could have done to my sister to cause this hatred. I would not even know where to begin. I asked to be shown why and yet have I come to see a sliver of what could cause this. It can only be evil, from a very dark place.

People have killed others for $100 or less. I really did not need another reason except greed. All the injustices that were done to me were for the gain of money. I had to forgive every person who had trespassed against me. I wondered why I needed all those traumatic experiences? I am on the beautiful journey of forgiveness. They certainly all showed me proof I would survive any amount of pain. I am sure of my power to heal and seal up wounds. It is what I came here to do.

I came to cleanse my karma and deal with all the pain. I also came to receive my bliss too. I am grateful to all the collaborating souls on my journey. The evolution of my soul is all that matters to me now. The main message I wanted to share that it has helped me heal in each moment of doubt and pain. Being alive is a privilege. God promises we will be loved and cared for by him. We must choose to receive his love, guidance, and protection. The Earth plane is not without suffering. The incredible point is to pass through the suffering and still praise our creator. I do this often and somehow it magically soothes my pain.

We are born to forget and live to remember. I have remembered so much through all of this pain about how great I am. I am a grain of sand, a leaf on the tree, a bird, an ant, a shimmer of hope. I will to power my soul each day. I have mastered the idea of me not controlling anything in my life. I cannot deny there is an invisible team of beings working to protect, guide, and love me. I am truly grateful to be breathing still.

I have a journey to complete and look forward to it. I believe in the light, source, water as creator, *God*. It is a predestined journey and I have done my best to love others and, most importantly, be compassionate. I will stand up for myself, when necessary. The most difficult lesson I am learning is self-love. I hated myself for a very long time with no real reason. It is an energy overlay I could not get out of my system no matter how hard I tried.

I had all the reasons to love myself and be proud, as I have accomplished so much. I have helped so many people. I finally see all of my accomplishments and impact I have made on people, children and animals. I love my soul so much. I removed the blocks and the dark energies that bound me to self-hate. I am a sovereign soul ready for what God has for me. My heart is filled with compassion and love for all sentient beings. I live for nature and natural settings. I am a warrior and will continue to fight for the light, the good, the rights of animals, others, and myself.

# FORGIVENESS IS FREEDOM

Seventeen years ago in 2006, I emailed my friends and family the question: What is Forgiveness to you? I saved all responses in a file. My younger sister responded: "Everyone has a story. One's life is a novel. Forgiveness is turning the page. Though, what is being forgiven will always remain in the chapter. You move forward and in time you process and make reason. Finally, the chapter closes and a new one begins."

My older sister responded: Peter came to Jesus and asked, "Lord, how many times shall I forgive my brother when he sins against me?"

"Up to seven times." Jesus answered. "I tell you, not seven times, but seventy-seven times (or seventy times seven)." Peter came to Jesus and asked.

Who would have thought in 2012, my two sisters would abandon me at the worse time in my life? This is the last page of the old chapter. My new chapter begins. I forgive and I am now am free. The question has been asked over and over: Why would God allow evil? The answer I came to understand is God will not intervene with a human's free will. God obscures himself to protect our destiny. If he were to appear on a regular basis, there would be no need for Faith. The purpose of free will is to allow the human experience in this realm and make choices according to their intuition and faith. This realm has many distractions, obstacles, and choices which, in essence, is the *human experience*. God at times, must intervene as he did with me several times. I escaped death, destruction, disability, and much more. He certainly sent his angels to cover me. I feel truly blessed to know I am loved. This life has shown me cruelty, trauma, and abuse. I could only be here today to write the words:

## GOD IS WATER! GOD IS LOVE! GOD IS EVERYWHERE!

The word water symbolizes salvation and eternal life, which God offers humankind through faith in his Son. All around me, throughout my journey, I came to know he is real and watching over us. This realm is the realm of cruelty, suffering, as well as the opposite, bliss, truth, beauty, and love live here too. As children of God, we are called the Human Race as we are all in a race to elevate into pure consciousness.

Death, fear, pain, trauma, all illusionary if put in the right perspective. There should be a singular quest for bliss, love, and connection. The cruelty and suffering keep this game of life in balance. The Garden of Eden is within all of us so we must choose with our free will to own the land. Some of us were forced out of the Garden of Eden as I was. I have been fighting ever since to return. Healing my mind, my soul, and my aura is what has immersed me. It has been a long, lonely journey for me. I have never been alone though, and this has been my solace.

My faith is in the unseen love and guidance of my creator. I have proof over and over we are part of an intricate, cosmic, well-oiled machinery of purpose, intention, and creation. It cannot be denied or hidden. All the fact the checkers in this realm do not stand a chance. I have witnessed and experienced the truth of all truths. I share with you the knowledge I have gained and this is my gift to you all. Suffering is not the end goal. You are to rise in faith and in this space, make sure all of your choices are from your heart. Do not fall victim of the dark forces of this realm. They tried to trick me, kill me, and take what is most valuable, *my* Faith! I never gave up my faith. The Demons were trying so hard to make me forget who I served.

# DIMENSION SHIFT: MY SPECIFIC HEALING TECHNIQUES AND DEVICES

Surrendering to God was an imperative part of my journey. I was free to just be and not worry about my thoughts or direction. I loved this part of my journey and I to this day I allowed Him to guide my path. I make choices with my soul in view. I used to make decisions only with my eyes or mental input. This is the conscious way to live in this realm. I am in tune with my heart as well. I seek to accelerate the beats of my heart. I created moments that invigorate a warm sensation through my energy field.

To see with your soul is to know with your faith, that (YOU) are the one you have been waiting for. To know thyself is the greatest quest that Hue-Mans have to embark upon. I am sure I requested this life and all that occurred to lead me to this level of consciousness. I am reveling in the consciousness of what is all around us. The clues are so clearly laid out before me.

When you can separate yourself from the experience, become the observer of your life, you will begin the true journey of self-discovery. I am a practitioner of the healing modality STT, Spontaneous

Transformation Technique. It is a simple yet effective technique that can release unwanted feeling in seconds. There is twelve-step walk through process that is done in the moment of being upset. It is the most effective technique I have found to calm the soul. When you are calm and free from emotions you can make better choices. You can actually control your machinery from this space of clarity.

# WATER QUOTES IN THE BIBLE

John 7:38
Jesus answered, "Truly, truly, I say to you, unless one is born of water and the Spirit, he cannot enter into the kingdom of God.

Psalm 1:3
He will be like a tree firmly planted by streams of water,
Which yields its fruit in its season
And its leaf does not wither;
And in whatever he does, he prospers

Isaiah 58:11
"And the LORD will continually guide you,
And satisfy your desire in scorched places,
And give strength to your bones;
And you will be like a watered garden,
And like a spring of water whose waters do not fail.

*My daily affirmations that keep my soul*
*purpose in alignment with GOD*

OPONOPONO Hawaiian MANTRA
I am sorry, please forgive me, I thank you, I love you

I am the possibility of all possibilities in this realm and all dimensions in the Galaxy

I am the light of the World grant me peace, love, joy and abundance

I pledge allegiance to Christ Consciousness today, tomorrow, forever and eternally.

God is Water, God is love, I am water, I am loved, I am God

I am a SOVEREIGN SOUL you have no control over me

# A ROMANTIC RELATIONSHIP WITH GOD

After writing this book, I actually see so much. I finally realized my life has been a relationship with God. I have been in a beautiful, well communicated relationship with him. We share deep love and compassion, more than I have ever known in my personal relationships on Earth. It is so strange to see it this way and only did I recognize it when I completed the book. God sent his best angels to protect, love, and guide me.

There were many experiences that were unavoidable, but throughout, he did not let me perish. It was not my time yet, thankfully. God sent me the most beautiful human love experiences too. The most beautiful gift of all was my perception or the ability to perceive His love and know it is real. I have collected memories and experiences to live out my destiny in such a beautiful way. I see this as a remarkable timeline journey. That is why I had the courage to share my personal trauma story with readers. I have come to understand free will vs. fate.

I discovered that my will has been stronger than most of the people I have encountered earlier in my life. I certainly exercised it at an early age. Will is the power of your soul to generate your reality. It is necessary to have a strong will to navigate this Earth plane. At the same time, I believe that we have a predestined journey and we utilized our will to get through the journey. I tried to manifest or will a new path, and it was not achieved.

I learned so much more by forging a path that was really not my destiny. In essence it was all perfectly set up. It has been said in many ways that trauma leads us to our real self. The persona we have created in childhood is forged by our environment, will eventually crumble. Humans will fight to keep the persona, yet eventually, we will break into pieces. We have to reorganize our existence and seek something higher. Seek it and do not run away from the source of your existence. I hope that everyone who reads this book truly acknowledges their life's journey. I want to encourage you to open your mind, clean up your diet, and go within. Meditate on your accomplishments and honor fully your authentic self. The connection to God is awaiting you.

# GOLDEN HUMAN GUIDED MEDITATION

I created a meditation to assist those who have experienced trauma in their lives. Those who have triggers that keep them feeling less than, weak, in patterns of lack and devaluation.

It came to me while I was meditating on how to keep in alignment with my new found self-love and confidence.

A vision came to me, seeing my body turned into a solid gold statue. Standing there looking beautiful, valuable and shiny. I then saw there were some tarnish marks, places where my trauma was stored. I looked at those tarnish spots and began to touch them and buff them out with a magic rub. I was healing my own wounds. I realized those tarnish spots are my weakness spot where others whom had seen them came to enter again and again to trigger my traumas. I see how I am responsible for using my self-love magic wand to buff out the tarnish and shine up my golden self to perfection.

# GOLDEN MANTRA MEDITATION

*Repeat*

I am valuable. I am solid. I am shiny. I am whole. I am precious. I am loved by me and others. I am worth my weight in Gold in all galaxies. My soul shines through my Golden Aura. The light of the universe is Powerfully Golden. I am the light of the universe. I can heal my wounds, past traumas and pain with the wave of my golden hand. I have the power of love to heal me and others. I prosper when I am solid, shiny and bright. Anyone who seeks to tarnish me, I will repel. I cover my soul with a Golden Cubed Aura frequency that reflects any negative intentions back to sender. I am in the Golden Light now and forever.